THE ULTIMATE BRAIN GAMES AND PUZZLES BOOK FOR TEENS

Tricky But Fun Brainteasers, Trivia Challenges, Crosswords, Word Searches And Much More To Keep Your Mind Young And Engaged

Donovan Ellis

CONTENTS

INTRODUCTION

Welcome to Brain Games For Teens!

Inside here are more than 100 fiendish puzzles, cryptograms, word games, brainteasers, and code solver puzzles, all designed to test your brainpower and puzzle-solving ability!

The puzzles and games here have been arranged in five sections, from easiest to hardest. First up, we have a simple **WARM-UP** area that introduces some of the games you'll be playing and how they work—along with a few tips and tactics you might need to solve them! After that, there's an **EASY LEVEL** section to get you started; a **MEDIUM LEVEL** section, which makes things a little tougher; a **HARD LEVEL** that will really begin to test your brainpower; and a final set of **EXPERT LEVEL** games for only the best puzzle-solvers to take on!

Don't worry if you get stuck along the way, though—at the back of the book you'll find all the solutions, arranged in simple numerical order.

Happy puzzling!

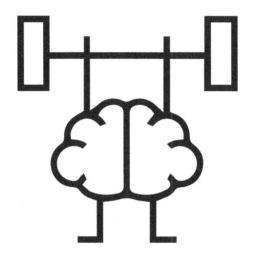

WARM-UP AREA

Take a few minutes to try out a few practice puzzles.

These will explain how to play all the main puzzles and games

for *Ultimate Brain Games and Puzzles Book for Teens*!

PRACTICE SECTION 1
CROSSWORD

There are lots of different kinds of crosswords inside *Brain Games for Teens*, from straightforward clue-solving games to anagram crosswords and number puzzles.

Solve them all in the usual way. The clues are divided into Across and Down, and are numbered in order throughout the grid. Fill in the answers letter by letter into the grid, starting from the corresponding numbered square.

Across answers read horizontally, and Down answers read vertically. Overlapping words will share the same letter in the connecting square.

Try this quick mini puzzle to get started.

Across

1. Argue noisily (8)

7. Riches, personal money (6)

8. Number in a pair (3)

9. People who make bread (6)

11. America is divided into 50 (6)

13. Damp, covered in water (3)

15. King Arthur's wizard (6)

16. Sport in which you might perform a front crawl (8)

Down

2. Makes a sound like a duck (6)

3. Theatrical performers (6)

4. Permit, allow (3)

5. How the animals entered Noah's Ark (3, 2, 3)

6. Romantic ballad (8)

10. Small river (6)

11. Taken without permission (6)

14. Pull or drag behind (3)

PRACTICE SECTION 2
WORDSEARCH

To solve a wordsearch you need to find all the listed clue words in the grid of jumbled letters. They can appear in any direction—forward or backward, upward or downward, horizontally, vertically, and diagonally.

Some of the clue words are split up, so you'll have to find **ALL** their individual parts in the grid. If a clue word were listed as **"WORD / SEARCH"**, for instance, you would have to find both **WORD** and **SEARCH** in the puzzle as separate answers.

Here's a quick mini puzzle to get you started. Can you find the names of all these superheroes in the grid below?

Antman

Batman

Black / panther

Black widow

Captain / marvel

Deadpool

Doctor / strange

Hawkeye

Hulk

Spiderman

Superman

Wolverine

Wonder / woman

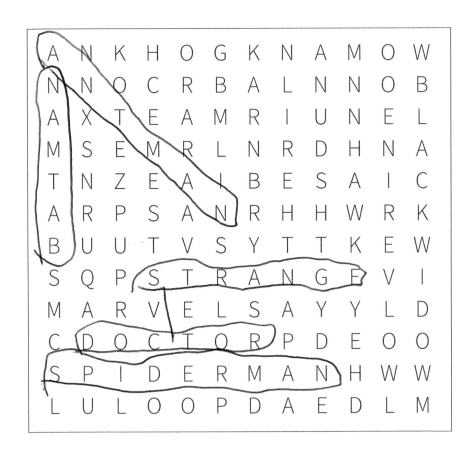

PRACTICE SECTION 3
CRYPTOGRAM

This is a cryptogram puzzle. All the letters in the well-known phrase below have been swapped for another letter of the alphabet.

A few of the letters have been given to you to start it off—so all of the Is have been swapped for Cs, all of the Ns have been swapped for Js, and all of the Hs have been swapped for Ds. Based on those, can you work out what the phrase actually says?

W   U C X Q   C J   E D N   D W J Q   C A   S I X E D

E S I   C J   E D N   U K A D

_   _ _ I _ _   IN   _ H _   H _ N _   I _   _ O _ _ H

_ _ O   IN   _ H _   _ _ _ _ H

PRACTICE SECTION 4
WORD PYRAMID

This is a word pyramid! Each of the answers to the seven clues contains the letters of the previous answer jumbled up, plus one new letter. A few of the letters have been filled in to help you. Can you solve the clues to complete the grid?

I

1.   I n   Not out

2.   _ _ _ _   Clear alcoholic spirit

3.   _ _ _ _ _   Wide smile

4.   _ _ _ _ _ I _   Farmer's crop; tiny amount

5.   _ _ G _ _ _ _   Get back

6.   _ _ _ _ _ _ _ G   Making money

7.   _ _ A _ _ _ _ _ _   Grandmothers

PRACTICE SECTION 5
CODEWORD

A codeword is a crossword with no clues! All the letters in the grid have been replaced with numbers—so A could be 1, B could be 2, and so on. All you have to do is figure out which number corresponds to which letter.

To do that, you'll be given a handful of letters in the correct places to get started, so right away you can go ahead and fill in all the numbers in the grid matching theirs. Then, based on how they fall into place, see how many of the other letters and words you can figure out and take it from there!

Use the alphabet and the reference grid below the main puzzle to keep track of which numbers and letters you've solved so far, and which are still left to work out.

Here's a quick game to get started. The letters of the word **QUOTE** are already in the grid. You can go ahead and fill in all the other Qs, Us, Os, Ts, and Es based on their numbers. Now what other words can you figure out from there?

13 Q	14	3	20	9		17		10	
14 U		15		3	18	3	12	3	11
4 O	12	12	9	11		24		22	
12 T		9		15	4	26	6	9	6
9 E	3	11		6		12		24	
	23		3		5		1	4	10
24	3	12	12	8	9		4		26
	22		12		19	3	21	9	2
11	9	16	26	25	9		9		2
	2		16		8	14	6	12	7

A B C D E F G H I J K L M N O P Q R S T U V W X Y Z

| 1 | 2 | 3 | 4 | 5 | 6 | 7 | 8 | 9 | 10 | 11 | 12 | 13 |
| 14 | 15 | 16 | 17 | 18 | 19 | 20 | 21 | 22 | 23 | 24 | 25 | 26 |

PRACTICE SECTION 6
ACROSTIC

In an acrostic puzzle, the answers to all the clues are the same length. Fill them into the grid in numerical order, top to bottom, into their corresponding rows. Some of the letters will be filled in already to help you make a start.

Once all the answers are written in the grid, a hidden phrase will be spelled out by the first letters of each word in order, reading top to bottom in the shaded column. It could be a saying, the title of a book, a place, a movie, a sporting event—anything at all! Find this hidden phrase to complete the puzzle.

Try this shorter 10-word game to get used to how to play.

1		I				
2				A		
3			C			
4				U		S
5				M		S
6		U		L		
7					N	D
8		X			R	
9			L		G	
10		N				E

1. London Heathrow or Chicago O'Hare, for example

2. American currency units

3. Type of sale in which buyers make rising bids

4. There are 60 of them in an hour!

5. Living creatures

6. Type of power station that uses uranium

7. Very hard precious stone

8. Search uncharted territory

9. Settlement smaller than a town

10. Make bigger, like a photograph

PRACTICE SECTION 7
Code Solver

This is a code solver puzzle. Here you're given a set of questions, the answers to which fit—letter by letter—into the numbered boxes below each one. Next, move each numbered letter into its corresponding box in the code on the opposite page. Once all the boxes are filled in, you'll spell out a famous quote!

So in the example below, the letters in the answer **BABOON** have been filled in at the bottom of the page in this famous quote from Shakespeare's *Macbeth*. Can you answer the remaining questions and crack the code?

1. What kind of monkey is known for its long hairless muzzle and sharp teeth?

$$1 \underline{B} \quad 2 \underline{A} \quad 3 \underline{B} \quad 4 \underline{O} \quad 5 \underline{O} \quad 6 \underline{N}$$

2. A long, spaghetti-like strand of dough cooked into Asian soups is called a…?

$$7 \underline{} \quad 8 \underline{} \quad 9 \underline{} \quad 10 \underline{} \quad 11 \underline{} \quad 12 \underline{}$$

3. What number is equal to one thousand billion—or 1 followed by 12 zeroes?

$$13 \underline{} \quad 14 \underline{} \quad 15 \underline{} \quad 16 \underline{} \quad 17 \underline{} \quad 18 \underline{} \quad 19 \underline{} \quad 20 \underline{}$$

4. What does a number 7 indicate on the pH scale?

$$21 \underline{} \quad 22 \underline{} \quad 23 \underline{} \quad 24 \underline{} \quad 25 \underline{} \quad 26 \underline{} \quad 27 \underline{}$$

5. What is a fragile metallic glass ball hung from a Christmas tree called?

$$28 \underline{} \quad 29 \underline{} \quad 30 \underline{} \quad 31 \underline{} \quad 32 \underline{} \quad 33 \underline{}$$

6. What 1997 sci-fi comedy movie starred Robin Williams as a scientist who creates a bright green, super-bouncy substance?

34 __ 35 __ 36 __ 37 __ 38 __ 39 __ 40 __

7. What word completes the title of the famous sitcom starring Larry David, ___ *Your Enthusiasm*?

41 __ 42 __ 43 __ 44 __

"D5 <u>O</u> 23 __ 28 __ 32 __ 39 __ ,

D8 __ 36 __ 1 <u>B</u> 11 __ 22 __ , 24 __ 9 __ 18 __ 16 __

26 __ 21 __ D 13 __ 43 __ 4 <u>O</u> 42 __ 44 __ 27 __ 33 __ ;

34 __ 15 __ 25 __ E 31 __ U 14 __ 6 <u>N</u> , 29 __ 20 __ D

41 __ 2 <u>A</u> 35 __ 10 __ 40 __ 19 __ 7 __

3 <u>B</u> 30 __ 38 __ 37 __ 17 __ 12 __ ."

---

❶ DID YOU KNOW?

Baboons are the world's largest monkeys. From the tops of their heads to the tips of their long tails, the largest species are more than 4½ft long!

PRACTICE SECTION 8
CRISSCROSS

In a crisscross puzzle, you're given all the answers! All you have to do is work out where in the grid they go. To do that, you'll need to keep track of how long each answer word is, and figure out where it goes based on where it connects to the surrounding words. To help, all the answers are listed by length. Try finding where all the unique answers go first of all—so in this sample puzzle of words to do with castle, there is only one six-letter word. Find that word first to make a start!

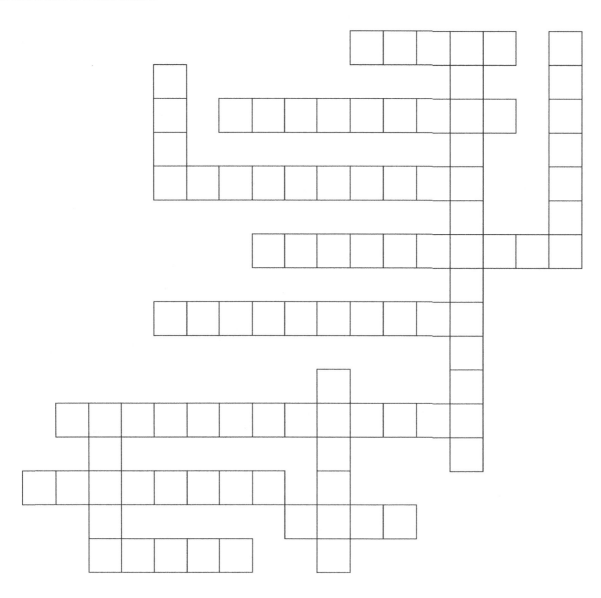

4 letters	5 letters	6 letters	7 letters	8 letters	9 letters	10 letters	13 letters
Keep	Arrow	Bailey	Turrets	Barbican	Loopholes	Battlement	Machicolation
Ward	Ditch					Drawbridge	Crenellations
	Walls					Portcullis	

PRACTICE SECTION 9
BRAINTEASERS

As well as all the usual puzzles and games here, there are also some unique brainteasers, the rules of each of which will be explained as we go along.

In this game, all the five-letter words below are missing one of their letters. Fill in the gaps to spell out a seven-letter word reading down the middle.

1.	BAC __ N	5.	__ NPUT
2.	__ TILL	6.	S __ ENE
3.	TO __ AL	7.	REAC __
4.	FAI __ Y		

PRACTICE SECTION 10
POP QUIZ

There are a few general knowledge quizzes mixed in along the way here too! Some of them will be themed, or might have a hidden clue that connects all their answers. Others—like the one below—will just be random trivia games! See how many you can get right…

1. The cities of Milan and Rome are in what European country?

2. Who is the headmaster of Hogwarts in the *Harry Potter* stories?

3. In what decade of the twentieth century did the First World War take place?

4. What item on a menu might be egg-fried, basmati, wholegrain, or sticky?

5. What is the only vowel on the middle row of a computer keyboard?

6. What kind of animal is a condor?

7. In what part of the body are there bones called the femur and the tibia?

8. Which of these planets has the most moons: Mars, Mercury, or Saturn?

9. What is the long spear thrown by an Olympic track and field athlete called?

10. Which English king famously had six wives?

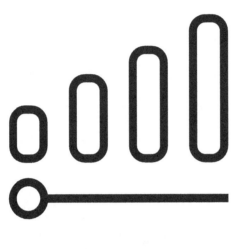

EASY

Now you're familiar with the rules, let's get things started.

This first section keeps things a little easier...

11

Place the answers to the clues on the right into the corresponding rows in the grid on the left, and the name of a popular movie franchise will be spelled out in the shaded column!

1. Leader of the United States

2. Very vital or essential

3. Outlaw who was friends with Friar Tuck

4. Koalas and kangaroos live here

5. Alexander Graham Bell's famous invention

6. Name of two famous English queens

7. Ninth month of the year

8. Clearly, needing no explanation

9. Rockets and Catherine wheels, for instance

10. Childhood stuffed toy resembling an animal

11. Filmmaking area of Los Angeles

12. Sudden difficult situation

13. Time of year you might sing carols

14. Exciting trip or journey

15. Author of *Matilda* and *The Witches*

16. Meeting with a future employer

17. The start, the commencement

18. German composer known for going deaf

19. Capital city of Scotland

20. ___ the Great was a famous figure from history

21. On a compass, it's opposite southwest

#								
1				I		E		
2		P						T
3							O	
4								A
5		L					N	
6								H
7						B		
8	B	V					L	
9				W			K	
10			D	Y				
11				Y	W			
12				G	E			Y
13								S
14		D	V			U		
15	R					D		
16						V		W
17		G						G
18				H		V		
19			N					H
20			X					
21		R				A		

❶ DID YOU KNOW?

That the author in the answer to CLUE 15 here wrote for four hours every day— in two two-hour slots, 10am-12pm and 2pm-4pm—in a small shed at the bottom of his garden!

12

Place the answers to the clues on the right into the corresponding rows in the grid on the left, and the name of a popular movie franchise will be spelled out in the shaded column!

Amsterdam
Antwerp
Athens
Bergen
Berlin
Bucharest
Budapest
Cannes
Cork
Dublin
Essen
Gdansk
Glasgow
Hamburg
Helsinki
Kiev
Lisbon
London
Madrid
Marseilles
Minsk
Moscow
Oslo
Paris
Riga
Rome

A	N	K	X	K	H	T	S	E	P	A	D	U	B	K
L	I	A	I	M	S	C	I	K	N	I	S	L	E	H
O	L	D	V	E	O	N	O	B	E	R	G	E	N	P
N	R	A	U	R	V	L	I	W	O	G	S	A	L	G
D	E	T	K	B	S	H	A	M	B	U	R	G	E	E
O	B	H	S	O	L	S	T	O	C	K	H	O	L	M
N	V	E	J	E	R	I	D	M	N	I	V	E	P	O
J	E	N	K	A	R	N	N	O	A	I	B	R	U	R
H	R	S	W	E	K	A	B	S	E	D	E	Q	R	C
W	O	C	S	O	M	S	H	N	I	W	R	I	U	A
F	N	X	P	E	I	O	N	C	T	R	G	I	V	N
R	A	Q	Z	L	N	A	O	N	U	A	A	W	D	N
V	A	L	E	N	C	I	A	H	L	B	Z	P	N	E
S	E	L	L	I	E	S	R	A	M	F	H	O	Q	S
A	M	S	T	E	R	D	A	M	G	D	A	N	S	K

Stockholm   Verona   Warsaw
Valencia   Vienna   Zagreb

❶ DID YOU KNOW?

The most populous city in Europe is Istanbul with 15 million inhabitants. But because the city straddles the Bosporus Strait at the mouth of the Black Sea, it actually lies in both Europe and Asia!

13

Across

1. Male spouse (7)

5. Things, random objects (5)

8. Coupon (7)

9. American horsemanship show (5)

10. Bump (5)

11. Serviettes (7)

12. Famous Parisian tower (6)

14. Clears the throat (6)

17. Six-sided shape (7)

19. Tubes (5)

22. Line from a song (5)

23. Not even, not fair (7)

24. Same again (5)

25. School tuition periods (7)

Down

1. Float in the air (5)

2. Noise (5)

3. Sportsman (7)

4. Extremely brave (6)

5. Leather tie (5)

6. Untying (7)

7. Cleans between the teeth (7)

12. Breathed out (7)

13. Ballroom dance named after an animal (7)

15. Dominate, hold back (7)

16. Yearly (6)

18. Lizard with gripping feet (5)

20. Planet downgraded in 2006 (5)

21. Pouts, huffs (5)

14

Can you decode this cryptogram to spell out a well-known saying?

G FHLDVNR HC BENDY G
DYEVCGPO BENOC

__ P____UR__ I__ ___R__H __

__H __US____ ___R__S

15

All the answers to this general knowledge quiz start with the same two letters. Once you've worked out what those are, some of the tougher questions should fall into place!

1. What chess piece can only move in diagonal lines across the board?

2. What kind of creature is a potoo?

3. What kind of deciduous hardwood tree is known for its thin, silvery bark?

4. In what number-matching game might you hear the call "legs eleven"?

5. What style of two-piece bathing unit is named after an island in the Pacific Ocean?

6. What is the number system of 1s and 0s that computers use called?

7. How is the famous clock at the top of the Elizabeth Tower in London's Westminster Palace better known?

8. The velocipede, the boneshaker, and the penny farthing were early forms of what form of transport?

9. What is a number 1 followed by nine zeroes called?

10. What is the scientific study of life and living organisms called?

11. What is the city of New York's famous fruity nickname?

12. How was the famous Wild West outlaw William Bonney better known?

ⓘ DID YOU KNOW?

*The outlaw who is the answer to **QUESTION 15** here might be better known by his nickname, but even his supposed "real" name, William H. Bonney, was a pseudonym. His birth name was actually Henry McCarthy!*

Grid (codeword puzzle):

	15 J	9 U	6 M	5 P	8	10	■	8	3	23	8	10
3	■	19	■	9	■	8	■	26	■	13	■	8
20	11	1	16	2	■	6	8	16	14	21	10	23
8	■	13	■	2	21	21	■	18	■	25	■	8
23	13	21	25	11	■	16	18	3	25	11	8	18
■	■	18	■	8	■	8	■	■	8	■	■	22
17	3	19	1	23	14	■	3	13	16	1	22	8
3	■	■	11	■	■	4	■	21	■	6	■	■
19	9	13	11	8	3	18	■	9	5	5	8	18
7	■	21	■	7	■	1	19	19	■	9	■	9
9	19	9	23	9	3	11	■	16	3	11	24	23
8	■	11	■	3	■	11	■	18	■	23	■	14
16	1	10	3	11	■	23	16	12	11	8	23	■

A B C D E F G H I J K L M N O P Q R S T U V W X Y Z

1	2	3	4	5	6	7	8	9	10	11	12	13
14	15	16	17	18	19	20	21	22	23	24	25	26

17

Place the answers to these questions letter by letter into the boxes, then move the letters into their corresponding boxes in the coded message below to reveal a famous opening line.

1. In literature, what kind of creature are Paddington, Rupert, and Winnie the Pooh?

1 __ 2 __ 3 __ 4 __ 5 __

2. What small pale brown seed is often served on top of hamburger buns?

6 __ 7 __ 8 __ 9 __ 10 __ 11 __

3. What North American mammal is the largest animal in the deer family?

12 __ 13 __ 14 __ 15 __ 16 __

4. What spooky name is given to an abandoned settlement, particularly in the Wild West of America?

17 __ 18 __ 19 __ 20 __ 21 __ 22 __ 23 __ 24 __ 25 __

5. In biology, what name is given to the complex process by which a cell replicates its chromosomes and splits in two to form two new cells with separate nuclei?

26 __ 27 __ 28 __ 29 __ 30 __ 31 __ 32 __

6. What completes the title of the famous piece of music by the Russian composer Rimsky-Korsakov, "The ___ of the Bumblebee"?

33 __ 34 __ 35 __ 36 __ 37 __ 38 __

7. What Roald Dahl story is about a horrible, spiteful husband and wife?

39 __ 40 __ 41 __ 42 __ 43 __ 44 __ 45 __ 46 __

8. What color comes between the blue and red stripes on the flag of France?

47 __ 48 __ 49 __ 50 __ 51 __

9. In what part of the body are there bones called metatarsals?

52 __ 53 __ 54 __ 55 __

10. One of what fraction is equal to 20%?

56 __ 57 __ 58 __ 59 __ 60 __

11. What is a female sheep called?

61 __ 62 __ 63 __

12. What is the Spanish word for goodbye?

64 __ 65 __ 66 __ 67 __ 68 __

"27 __ 21 __   62 __ 3 __ 15 __   28 __ 48 __ 7 __

1 __ 41 __ S 55 __   19 __ 33 __

39 __ 44 __ 12 __ 51 __ 46 __ ,   49 __ 22 __

W 9 __ 68 __   59 __ 18 __ E   W 29 __ 4 __ 6 __ T

23 __ 56 __   38 __ I 26 __ 11 __ S ,   31 __ T

47 __ A 20 __   42 __ 37 __ 63__

64 __ 36 __ 16__   13 __ F

24 __ 66 __ 30 __ 65 __ 53 __ 10 __ ,   35 __ 50 __

45 __ AS   45 __ 40 __ 2 __

A 17 __ 61 __   67 __ 58 __

52 __ 54 __ 14 __ 34 __ 57 __ 8 __ 60 __ 25 __ E 25 __ 32 __ ..."

18

SPOT THE 12 DIFFERENCES

19

Fill in the answers to the clues on the right into the grid on the left and the name of a famous landmark will read down the shaded column.

1. Smaller, less large

2. Time of day between afternoon and night

3. It's written on an envelope

4. Not one of two alternatives

5. Period of history that followed the Bronze Age (4, 2)

6. City where you can visit Times Square (3, 4)

7. Wizard in the *Lord of the Rings* and *The Hobbit*

8. Second day of the working week

9. These Games are held every four years

10. Type of movie that features cowboys

11. People who know a lot about certain subjects

12. Name of England's famous Lionheart king

13. Month when Halloween is celebrated

14. Monica, Rachel, Phoebe, Ross, Joey and Chandler in the famous TV sitcom

15. Secret, not open to outsiders

16. Volcanic island country in northern Europe

17. Homer and Bart's surname

18. They come after questions!

#						
1		T				
2	V					
3					S	
4		I				
5	R			A		
6		W				
7						F
8	U					
9		Y				
10	E	S				
11	X					S
12		C				
13				B		R
14	R		E			
15			V		T	
16	C					D
17	I					
18					R	

20

S

1.	__ __	I am, you are, it __
2.	__ __ __	Title of a knight
3.	__ __ __ __	Mix up
4.	__ __ __ __ P __	Journeys out
5.	S __ __ __ __ __	Movie screenplay
6.	__ A __ __ __ A __	Arm muscles
7.	S __ __ __ __ __ S	Images

21

The word on the left can have a letter added onto the end of it that the word on the right can have added onto the beginning of it! So in the first example, **EASTER** can gain a final N to make **EASTERN**, and **EVER** can gain an initial N to make **NEVER**. Place the extra letter in the box in the middle, and the name of a famous newspaper will be spelled out reading downward.

1.	EASTER	N	EVER
2.	PLEAS	__	QUIP
3.	NO	__	HEN
4.	EARL	__	OURS
5.	PEDAL	__	RANGE
6.	BREATHE	__	ANGER
7.	IN	__	NOT
8.	FIRS	__	HEM
9.	TAX	__	DEAL
10.	REAL	__	ALES
11.	BROWS	E	VENTS
12.	DISCUS	__	HALL

22

How many of these household fixtures and fittings can you find in the grid below?

```
X  J  E  U  D  S  R  I  A  H  C  M  R  A  M
G  A  B  L  E  T  E  C  U  P  B  O  A  R  D
W  F  R  L  B  N  O  T  B  L  A  N  K  E  T
A  D  E  T  E  A  A  I  T  E  F  F  U  O  P
S  R  A  A  L  M  T  K  L  E  E  Z  A  D  X
H  A  K  E  B  Q  K  G  F  E  E  Z  E  H  B
B  O  F  S  U  W  E  L  N  R  T  B  P  A  F
A  B  A  W  O  D  E  S  C  I  E  Y  T  Z  R
S  E  S  O  D  H  U  O  A  L  N  H  E  O  I
I  D  T  D  S  B  U  Y  G  C  T  I  V  T  D
N  I  B  N  A  C  C  N  A  U  K  E  D  I  G
X  S  A  I  H  Z  I  R  B  C  N  O  S  R  E
D  F  R  W  M  S  K  W  A  R  D  R  O  B  E
T  E  P  R  A  C  N  O  T  U  O  F  F  B  Y
K  I  T  C  H  E  N  T  A  B  L  E  A  B  I
```

Armchair	Couch	Oven	Sofa
Bathtub	Cupboard	Pouffe	Toilet
Blanket	Dining table	Settee	Wardrobe
Bookcase	Double bed	Shelf	Washbasin
Breakfast bar	Fridge	Sideboard	Window seat
Carpet	Kitchen table	Single bed	

---

❶ DID YOU KNOW?

Shakespeare used the word bedroom just once in all of his plays, in A Midsummer Night's Dream. He didn't use it as we would, though—he used it to mean the amount of room you have in your bed!

23

We're keeping things warm (or cold, as the case may be with gazpacho!) for this crisscross puzzle all about soups and stews.

4 letters
Crab
Fish
Stew

5 letters
Broth
Gumbo

6 letters
Barley
Bisque
Carrot
Lentil
Noodle
Oxtail

7 letters
Borscht
Chicken
Lobster
Seafood
Spinach
Tarator

8 letters
Chestnut
Chick pea
Consommé
Cucumber
Gazpacho
Mushroom
Split pea

9 letters
Bird's Nest
Pea and Ham
Vegetable

10 letters
Minestrone

11 letters
Cullen skink
French onion

18 letters
Broccoli and Stilton

24

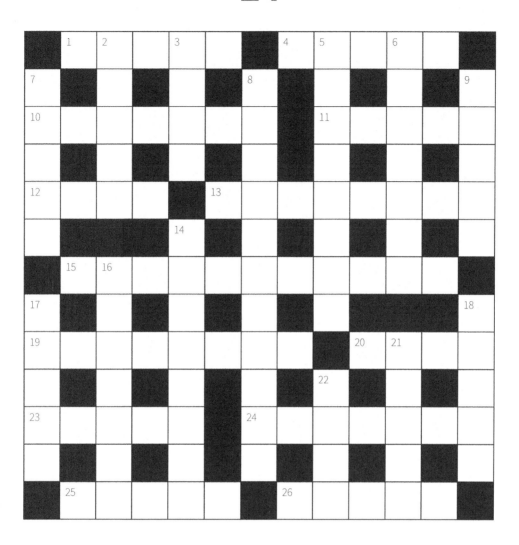

Across

1. People who work in a business (5)

4. Uttered, said (5)

10. Surrounded on either side (7)

11. Silk-like fabric (5)

12. Swerve, move off course (4)

13. Completed (8)

15. Alpine country in central Europe (11)

19. Fall down (8)

20. Continent on which the Himalayas are found (4)

23. Dog (5)

24. Polite demand (7)

25. Shows the way (5)

26. Tabletop lights (5)

Down

2. Name of a book (5)

3. Tiny blood-sucking insect (4)

5. Feasible, could happen (8)

6. Room for cooking (7)

7. Overhead, on top of (5)

8. Yearly commemoration of a wedding (11)

9. Unpleasant, mean; anagram of dines (5)

14. Connected (8)

16. Warm greeting (7)

17. Range (5)

18. Celebration (5)

22. Water; pop group who sang "Barbie Girl" (4)

25

Place the answers to these questions letter by letter into the boxes, then move the letters into their corresponding boxes in the coded message at the bottom of the page to reveal a famous quote from JRR Tolkien's *The Hobbit*.

1. Where would you find the Sea of Tranquillity?

1 __ 2 __ 3 __ 4 __

2. What is the surname of Justin, the popstar whose hits include "Despacito"?

5 __ 6 __ 7 __ 8 __ 9 __ 10 __

3. In what sport might you score a birdie?

11 __ 12 __ 13 __ 14 __

4. What is a period of 10 years known as?

15 __ 16 __ 17 __ 18 __ 19 __ 20 __

5. In the Bible, who killed Goliath with his slingshot?

21 __ 22 __ 23 __ 24 __ 25 __

6. Which famous Nelson was the president of South Africa from 1994 to 1999?

26 __ 27 __ 28 __ 29 __ 30 __ 31 __ 32 __

7. Baseball originally evolved from what simple bat-and-ball game, popular in England since the 1700s?

33 __ 34 __ 35 __ 36 __ 37 __ 38 __ 39 __ 40 __

8. How many chambers are there in a human heart?

41 __ 42 __ 43 __ 44 __

9. What wood is traditionally used to make cricket bats?

45 __ 46 __ 47 __ 48 __ 49 __ 50 __

10. What white Japanese curd made from soya beans is a popular vegan and vegetarian food?

51 __ 52 __ 53 __ 54 __

11. What kind of creature is a palomino?

55 __ 56 __ 57 __ 58 __ 59 __

12. What is a fence-like boundary made from closely grown bushes called?

60 __ 61 __ 62 __ 63 __ 64 __

"6 __ 41 __   1 __ 34 __ 33 __ 20 __   3 __ 14 __

43 __ 58 __   V 27 __ 31 __ 35 __ 30 __ 25 __

53 __ 2 __ 49 __ 19 __   22 __ 36 __ D

17 __ 55 __ 61 __ 64 __ 10 __   A 28 __ 62 __

40 __ O 4 __ 11 __   32 __ 8 __ 42 __ 23 __ 16 __

60 __ 52 __ A __ 44 __ 29 __ 7 __ D

62 __ 12 __ 13 __ 37 __ ,   24 __ 51 __

45 __ O 54 __ 48 __ 21 __   5 __ 59 __   18 __

26 __ 38 __ R 39 __ 46 __ 9 __ R

50 __ 56 __ 57 __ 47 __ 15 __."

26

All the five-letter words below are missing one of their letters. Fill in the gaps to spell out a 12-letter word reading down the middle.

1.	A __ OPT	7.	M __ SIC
2.	VAL __ D	8.	A __ TER
3.	CRA __ T	9.	HAS __ E
4.	O __ TEN	10.	V __ VID
5.	__ NDEX	11.	__ AGLE
6.	__ OMMA	12.	LO __ ER

27

QUIZ

1. Who sang the theme tune for the James Bond movie *Skyfall*?

2. In what European city is the Eiffel Tower?

3. What was the name of the British queen who ruled for most of the 19th century?

4. How many strings does a standard guitar have?

5. What is the name of the annual prizes that are awarded in the fields of physics, chemistry, physiology or medicine, literature, and peace?

6. Which ancient empire had rulers named Ramesses, Tutankhamun, and Cleopatra?

7. What kind of woodland creature lives in a burrow called a sett?

8. What is a measurement of eight pints known as?

9. The islands of Cuba and Jamaica lie in which sea?

10. What team sport uses wickets, stumps, and bails?

28

Place the answers to these questions letter by letter into the numbered boxes, then move the same letters into their corresponding boxes in the coded message below to reveal a famous line by the poet Edgar Allan Poe.

1. In what classic board game are there Chance cards and Community Chests?

1 __ 2 __ 3 __ 4 __ 5 __ 6 __ 7 __ 8 __

2. Well known for her beauty, who was Queen of Egypt from 51 to 30 BCE?

9 __ 10 __ 11 __ 12 __ 13 __ 14 __ 15 __ 16 __ 17 __

3. What type of insect spreads malaria?

18 __ 19 __ 20 __ 21 __ 22 __ 23 __ 24 __ 25 __

4. What kind of geographical feature has an opening called a vent?

26 __ 27 __ 28 __ 29 __ 30 __ 31 __ 32 __

5. What is the English translation of the Spanish phrase "fin de semana"?

33 __ 34 __ 35 __ 36 __ 37 __ 38 __ 39 __

6. What are elephants' tusks made from?

40 __ 41 __ 42 __ 43 __ 44 __

7. A member of Canada's Royal Canadian Mounted Police would be known by what nickname?

45 __ 46 __ 47 __ 48 __ 49 __ 50 __ 51 __

8. What is the first name of former *Spider-Man* actor and Oscar nominee Garfield?

52 __ 53 __ 54 __ 55 __ 56 __ 57 __

9. Calligraphy is the art of especially fine what?

58 __ 59 __ 60 __ 61 __ 62 __ 63 __ 64 __ 65 __ 66 __ 67 __ 68 __

10. What is the surname of the famous Victorian English scientist?

69 __ 70 __ 71 __ 72 __ 73 __ 74 __ 75 __

"2 __ 53 __ 29 __ 34 __   22 __ 13 __ 12 __N   30 __

45 __ 66 __ 73 __ 3 __ 40 __ G 58 __ 15 __

39 __ 63 __ 11 __ A 43 __ 44 __ , 33 __ H 64 __ 7 __ 51 __

23 __   5 __ 19 __ 48 __ 54 __ E 71 __ 37 __ D

62 __ 56 __ 72 __ 36 __   52 __ 60 __ D

57 __ 35 __ 59 __ 16 __ 8 __ ,   /

27 __ 41 __ E 55 __   1 __ 70 __ 38 __ 75 __   14 __

21 __ U 74 __ 50 __ N 49 __   17 __ 67 __ 61 __

9 __ 47 __ R I 4 __ U 20 __   __ 26 __ 32 __ 28 __ U 18 __ E

25 __ F   69 __ 46 __ R 68 __ 6 __ 65 __ 24 __ E 31 __

10 __ 42 __ R E ..."

29

Tea and coffee are the theme of this wordsearch!

```
T  H  P  E  P  P  E  R  M  I  N  T  L  A  R
J  E  S  O  S  S  E  R  P  S  E  A  V  C  E
K  A  A  I  A  H  C  O  M  Y  B  A  U  E  C
E  A  P  P  L  K  E  U  M  R  J  B  J  R  U
T  H  N  A  O  G  B  R  E  W  I  N  G  E  A
T  C  O  I  N  T  N  H  P  A  R  L  T  M  S
L  A  E  T  H  E  R  E  I  A  A  K  S  O  D
E  P  N  N  W  C  S  L  W  T  G  H  A  N  N
S  P  I  Y  O  A  E  E  T  O  U  F  F  Y  A
T  U  E  F  M  M  T  E  S  M  S  O  K  P  P
E  C  F  A  A  O  E  E  I  N  O  B  A  U  U
A  C  F  C  S  M  Z  L  R  L  A  N  E  R  C
M  I  A  E  S  I  K  X  O  Y  L  E  R  Y  Q
E  N  C  D  A  L  G  N  I  L  I  O  B  S  X
D  O  Y  Z  S  E  G  Y  E  R  G  L  R  A  E
```

Assam	Camelia	Earl grey	Java	Peppermint
Beans	Camomile	English	Kettle	Steamed / Milk
Boiling	Cappuccino	Espresso	Latte	Sugar
Breakfast	China	Herbal	Lemon	
Brewing	Cup and saucer	Hot water	Mocha	Syrup
Caffeine	Decaf	Japanese / Ceremony	Oolong	Teapot

ⓘ DID YOU KNOW?

That tea is traditionally made from the leaves of just one plant, Camelia sinensis, which is native to a tiny region on the border of India and China.

30

Fit the answers to the clues on the right into the corresponding rows on the left and the name of a famous fairy story will read down the shaded column.

1. Cinema secret agent Mr. Bond

2. Someone who performs on stage

3. Country of which Beijing is the capital

4. Eucalyptus-eating marsupial

5. A right __ has 90 degrees

6. It follows day

7. Take in liquid

8. Contemplate, mull over

9. Place where paying guests stay the night

10. When a premature person might arrive

11. Highest value ball in a game of snooker

12. Message in a computer's inbox

13. Large metal block struck by a blacksmith

14. More pleasant, better behaved

15. Twig

16. Sum of a series of numbers or amounts

17. Fruit that can be a Granny Smith or a Pink Lady

18. Nearby, in the surrounding area

19. Male monarchs

#					
1					S
2		C			
3			I		
4					A
5		N			
6					
7					K
8					K
9					L
10					Y
11		L			
12					
13			V		
14			C		
15		T			K
16			T		
17					
18		O		A	
19		I			

31

A

1. __ __   Dad

2. __ __ __   Ideal golf score

3. __ __ __ __   Set of two

4. __ __ P __ __   Jungle animal with a long snout

5. P __ __ __ __ __ __   Swashbuckling treasure seeker

6. __ __ __ N __ __ __   Artist

7. __ __ __ __ __ P __ __   Turtle-like reptile

32

Can you decode this cryptogram to spell out a famous proverb?

N C   N V V H W   N   G N S   Z W W V M   B Q W
G J O B J X   N I N S

A_ A_____ A _A_ _____S ___

_O__O_ A_A_

33

SPOT THE SIX DIFFERENCES

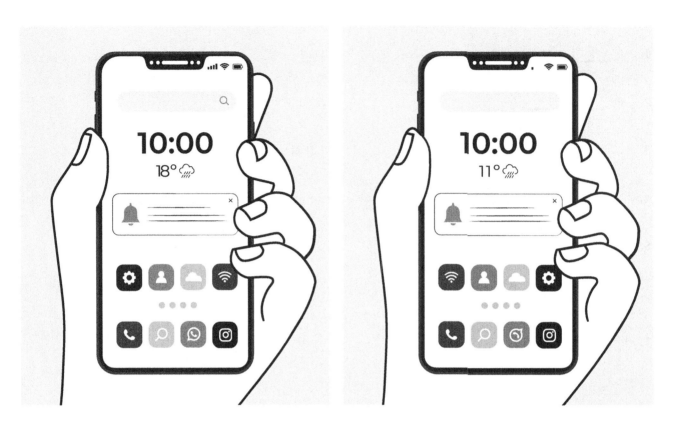

34

All the answers to the questions in this general knowledge quiz begin and end with the same two letters. Once you know what they are, you might be able to work out some of the tougher ones!

1. What is a group of lions called?
2. Which classic cartoon character is the boyfriend of Olive Oyl?
3. What kind of falcon is the fastest bird in the world?
4. What is the official language of Brazil?
5. What is the flat wooden handheld board used by an artist to mix their paints called?
6. Elizabeth Bennett is a character in what classic English novel by Jane Austen?
7. What famous make of car has a picture of a black horse on its badge?
8. What flat round dish made of lightly cooked batter is traditionally eaten on Shrove Tuesday?
9. Violet is a shade of what color?
10. What is the name of the artistic technique in which objects are drawn at different sizes to create an illusion of depth in a painting, and give the impression that one is further away than another?
11. What is the capital of the Czech Republic?
12. What title is held by the son of a king and queen?

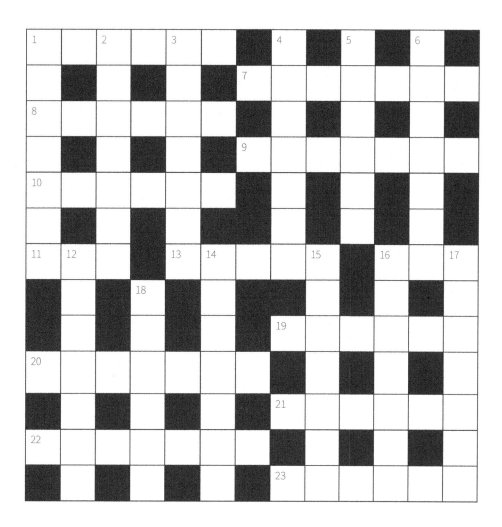

Across

1. Get back (6)
7. Confidentiality, secrecy (6)
8. Area surrounded by water (6)
9. Policeman (7)
10. Baas like a sheep (6)
11. For what reason? (3)
13. From the point that (5)
16. Brewed hot drink (3)
19. Talkative bird (6)
20. Moves continuously and nervously (7)
21. Plays a guitar (6)
22. Bendy yellow fruits (7)
23. Constricting snake (6)

Down

1. Arc in the sky (7)
2. Art museum (7)
3. Lights on fire (7)
4. Road congestion (7)
5. Dodges (7)
6. Physics or chemistry, for example (7)
12. Vacation (7)
14. First letter (7)
15. Precisely (7)
16. By way of (7)
17. Craftsperson, creative maker (7)
18. Native American dwelling (7)

36

Fill in the answers to the clues on the right into the corresponding boxes on the left, and a familiar phrase will be spelled out in the shaded column.

1. Skill, natural or learned ability

2. Famous play by William Shakespeare

3. Number that is the square root of 121

4. Size between small and large

5. Legendary character who supposedly flew too close to the sun

6. First name of *Harry Potter* actor Radcliffe

7. Scientist known for his theory of evolution

8. Portable set of steps for reaching up a height

9. Continent where Spain and Italy are found

10. English city famous for its ancient university

11. Device used to pour liquid into a narrow container without spilling it

12. Most modern, most recent

13. Connected to the internet

14. Giant marine mammals

15. Occurring every 60 minutes

16. Sufficient, just the right amount

17. Come back

18. Sticky yellow substance naturally produced in the ear canal

#					
1		L			
2					T
3					
4					
5				U	S
6	A				
7			W		
8					R
9					
10	X				
11					L
12		W			
13	N				
14	H				
15			R		
16					H
17			U		
18			W		

ℹ️ DID YOU KNOW?

*That icky substance that is the answer to **QUESTION 18** here has a proper name—it's called cerumen.*

37

We're heading to a restaurant for this wordsearch puzzle. How many of these 25 food and drink terms can you find below?

```
P P K C X N U C W V T W S N B
T Y R R O R A A E R S I I O E
Y S G E E N T G E S K N D I V
C W U T H E D S E S R E E T E
Z R I R R T S I N V O L D A R
T A I A R E O O M P F I I V A
W R V T D C O L S E S S S R G
F N A S I P S X C A N T H E E
K L U Y S C S E V E U T E S S
G L A S S E S K V M L C S E H
P S E L B A T F V I H B E R T
A P P E T I Z E R A N O A S H
K I T C H E N T I B Q K D T G
D O O F A E S R U O C N I A M
H G I W F I S H K N I F E B E
```

Appetizer	Dessert	Knives	Side dishes	Trays
Beverages	Fish knife	Main course	Spoons	Vegan
Chair	Forks	Reservation	Starter	Waiter
Condiments	Glasses	Sauces	Tablecloth	Water
Critics	Kitchen	Seafood	Tables	Wine list

ⓘ DID YOU KNOW?

The world's biggest restaurant is the Damascus Gate in Syria. It has 6,014 seats!

38

Place the answers to these questions letter by letter into the boxes, then move the letters into their corresponding boxes in the coded message at the bottom of the page to reveal a famous political quotation.

1. *The Two Towers* is the second book in what famous fantasy trilogy?

1 __ 2 __ 3 __ 4 __ 5 __ 6 __ 7 __ 8 __ 9 __ 10 __

11 __ 12 __ 13 __ 14 __ 15 __ 16 __ 17 __

2. What liquid measurement is abbreviated to "tsp."?

18 __ 19 __ 20 __ 21 __ 22 __ 23 __ 24 __ 25 __

3. What is the proper name for the formal crowning of a new British monarch?

26 __ 27 __ 28 __ 29 __ 30 __ 31 __ 32 __ 33 __ 34 __ 35 __

4. In what Scottish city is The Royal Mile a famous thoroughfare?

36 __ 37 __ 38 __ 39 __ 40 __ 41 __ 42 __ 43 __ 44 __

5. What chemical element has the symbol B?

45 __ 46 __ 47 __ 48 __ 49 __

6. What was the first name of the famous Dutch artist Van Gogh?

50 __ 51 __ 52 __ 53 __ 54 __ 55 __ 56 __

7. What country was once ruled by Napoleon Bonaparte and King Louis XIV?

57 __ 58 __ 59 __ 60 __ 61 __ 62 __

8. In what 2000 film did Tom Hanks play a man stranded on a desert island after a plane crash?

63 __ 64 __ 65 __ 66 __ 67 __ 68 __ 69 __ 70 __

9. How many make a baker's dozen?

71 __ 72 __ 73 __ 74 __ 75 __ 76 __ 77 __ 78 __

10. What word for a holiday keepsake literally means "to remember" in French?

79 __ 80 __ 81 __ 82 __ 83 __ 84 __ 85 __ 86 __

"57 __ 27__ 41 __ 86   17 __ 26 __ 34 __ 6 __E

20 __ 55__ 37 __   65 __ 19__ 50 __ 76 __ 15 __

Y54 __ 64 __ 13 __ 79 __   67 __ 43 __ 5 __

23 __ U74   F59 __ 1 __ 72 __77 __ 28 __ 21 __

40 __ 42 __ 48 __ 81 __ 16 __ 11 __ 66 __

9 __ 29__ 47 __ 32 __ 44 __ ,

U22 __ 8 __ 84 __   75 __ 2 __ 38 __S

63 __ 24 __ 35 __ 56 __ 51 __ 25 __ 62 __ 39 __ 10 __ ,

69 __   78 __ 36__ 68 __

52 __ 31 __ 18 __ 14 __ 80 __ 60 __ ,

61 __ 46 __ 30 __ 53 __ 12 __ 73 __ 82 __ 83 __ 7 __

85 __ 49 __ 4 __ 33 __ 45 __ 3 __ 58 __ 71 __ 70 __ …"

13	15	9	21	15	15	13		9	6	4	15	18
17		26		10		6		6		17		8
3	15	2	21	6		18	16	26	15	6	20	18
3		17		9		23		12		7		12
8	6	9	23	12		15	4	17	18	24	13	15
		1				13		24				14
15	11	15(E)	(C)	12(T)	18(S)		6	7	5	15	1	18
19			24		14				6			
19	6	21	6	22	6	8		6	4	21	24	7
24		17		6		18		1		1		17
21	15	25	15	21	18	15		24	7	17	24	7
12		15		13		1		7		15		15
18	24	21	12	18		19	17	5	26	21	15	18

A	N
B	O
C	P
D	Q
E	R
F	S
G	T
H	U
I	V
J	W
K	X
L	Y
M	Z

1	11	21
2	12	22
3	13	23
4	14	24
5	15	25
6	16	26
7	17	
8	18	
9	19	
10	20	

40

Can you decode this cryptogram to spell out a famous proverb?

FEY'D AEXYD TEXP AVCAUOYJ
IOHEPO DVOT VSDAV

_O_'_ _O_N_ _O___ _H_____S

___FO___ _____ HA___H

MEDIUM

Now that you're up and running, let's make things a little tougher!

41

Place the answers to the clues in the corresponding rows to spell out a famous couple from history reading downward in the shaded column.

1. Personal profile on social media

2. Large country in western Africa

3. In the direction of (UK spelling)

4. Month in which a Libra or a Scorpio might be born

5. Badly behaved

6. Less old

7. It's found by adding up a series of values, then dividing the total by the number of values you started with

8. Spotted, paid attention to

9. Illness

10. Flow of electricity

11. Famous US president, Abraham ___

12. Vibrating membrane involved in hearing sound

13. City in Florida that's home to Walt Disney World

14. Kind of figure that represented by the symbol %

15. Permitted, let happen

16. Poorly youngster in Charles Dickens' *A Christmas Carol* (4, 3)

17. Language you might ear spoken in Moscow

18. Amazing! Wonderful!

#							
1		C	C				
2							A
3			W				
4		C					
5							Y
6					G		R
7		V					
8			T		C		
9			S			S	
10				R			
11			N				
12							M
13							O
14				C			
15		L	L				
16				Y			
17				S	I		
18		W					

ℹ DID YOU KNOW?

Charles Dickens' Christmas Carol was written in a flurry of activity in 1843. He came up with the idea behind the book after attending a fundraising charity gala in Manchester in October, and completed the entire work within just six weeks. It went on sale the following December, and sold out in just three days!

42

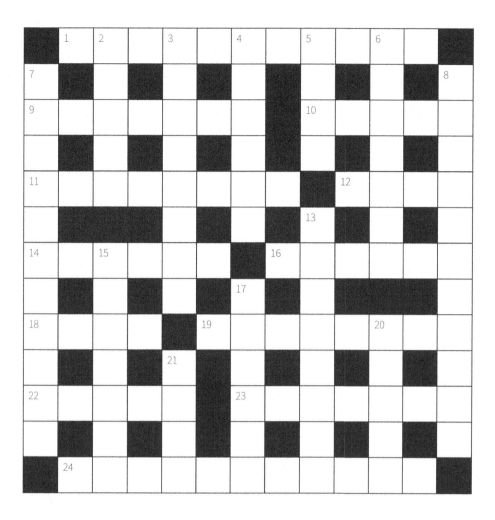

Across

1. See-through (11)
9. Gave another title (7)
10. Subject of a conversation (5)
11. Nose holes (8)
12. Melody (4)
14. Warm (4, 2)
16. Up to date (6)
18. Destroy completely (4)
19. Marine, relating to the sea (8)
22. Go in (5)
23. __ Awards, the Oscars (7)
24. High-ranking clergymen (11)

Down

2. Places in order of superiority (5)
3. Plentiful (8)
4. Foot-operated levels (6)
5. Rodents, vermin (4)
6. Outermost planet (7)
7. They're often served with hamburgers (6, 5)
8. Movie scripts (11)
13. Outdoor walkway (8)
15. Pilot (7)
17. Wildlife-watching trek (6)
20. Inexpensive (5)
21. Curved structure (4)

43

We're heading beneath the waves for this wordsearch puzzle! How many of these watery words and marine animals can you find below?

```
C M G R K S L Y E E T A N A M
R L A R O C U L M A L G A E E
A U A L B A T R O S S T C S L
B H T E N N A G F T Q N R T E
S E D I T P I R S B A I O U C
H A M M E R H E A D O P P A T
Y V O H C N A R S E S A O R R
N A Q W W S R H L B E R R Y I
I Q Q A N A O I B E V R P D C
H Q R A C R D H G A A E O D E
P P K U E O D E P C W T I P E
L E D L C P M I R H S P S B L
O A I O F I S H I N G N E T A
D N R S U M A T O P O P P I H
E C D B Z A L L I G A T O R W
```

Albatross	Coral	Fishingnet	Porpoise	Shrimp
Algae	Crab	Gannet	Prawn	Surfboard
Alligator	Crocodile	Hammerhead	Riptide	Terrapin
Anchovy	Dolphin	Hippopotamus	Sea snake	Turtle
Atoll	Electric eel	Manatee	Shark	Waves
Barracuda	Estuary	Orca	Shoreline	Whale
Beach				

ⓘ DID YOU KNOW?

Electric eels can grow up to 2½m (8ft) long, and can produce an electric shock of up to 860 volts!

44

E

1.	__ __	Spanish 'the'
2.	__ __ __	Beer
3.	__ __ __ L	Marine mammal
4.	__ __ __ __ __	Artist's stand for their canvas
5.	__ S __ __ __ __	Slumbering, not awake
6.	__ E __ __ P __ __	Suffer a previous medical complaint
7.	P __ E __ __ __ __	Enjoyment

45

The name of a different fruit is hidden somewhere inside each of these sentences—even between different words, as in the first example! How many of them can you spot?

1. Look at the **man go**ing to work!   **MANGO**

2. Can you hand me my cap, please?   _____

3. Gabriel was a more senior angel!   _____

4. We need to swap ricotta cheese for mozzarella!   _____

5. Grab an anaconda!   _____

6. The teacher Ryan liked was leaving.   _____

7. He's recording rap, especially hip-hop!   _____

8. Back I will go!   _____

46

SPOT THE SIX DIFFERENCES

47

Can you decode this cryptogram to spell out a famous piece of proverbial advice?

PIM'O HAPKZ D UIIF UX
LOR NIGZW

_O_'T J__E _ _OO_ ___
_T_ _O_E_

48

Place the answers to the clues in the corresponding rows in the grid, and a set of famous legendary characters will appear in the shaded column.

1. A computer has one—and so does a piano!
2. Games company that makes the Wii and Switch
3. Wounds
4. Placing bets, wagering money
5. Schoolwork you don't finish in school!
6. Day of the week named after the Norse god Thor
7. Timetable, order of events
8. US state that shares its name with a famous stage musical
9. The 14th of this month is Valentine's Day
10. Country whose capital is Bangkok
11. Surname of George, one of the four Beatles in the famous pop group
12. Scientist famous for the equation e = mc2
13. Hollywood actor Ryan
14. Normal, everyday
15. The entire cosmos
16. Main gas in the Earth's air
17. Linear measurement between two points
18. The day after today
19. Quarrel, noisy disagreement
20. Racket sport played on a diamond
21. Arabic or Swahili, for instance
22. It's the E in EU

#	(shaded)							
1		Y						
2								O
3		J						
4		M	B					
5				W				K
6	H							
7	C	H						
8	K							A
9							R	Y
10	H							D
11		R	R					
12	I							N
13		Y						S
14		D						Y
15		I						E
16	I							
17		S		A				
18								W
19		G			E			
20				B				
21			G					
22	U							N

49

Orchestras and instruments are the theme of this musical wordsearch.

```
C E L E S T E P E P N T E N P
B A S E E E I N H T A E U R C
Q A M W A C O G R L G N P O F
L N T L C H W U O Y R I H H L
W A O O P D M R E N O R O H U
V I L O N P O T O T G A N C T
V O X P E A B U T O T L I N E
H A Z T C X O I B E L C U E O
S B A S S O O N N L B L M R B
V I O L I N R O A A E L E F P
K U Q E Y E R N X I P B Z C J
O P F K M H E F E P P M A I C
B R K C O N D U C T O R I S S
O A N R O H H S I L G N E T S
E H N S L L E B R A L U B U T
```

Bassoon	Double bass	Oboe	Timpani
Baton	English horn	Organ	Trumpet
Celeste	Euphonium	Piano	Tuba
Cello	Flute	Piccolo	Tubular bells
Clarinet	French horn	Saxophone	Viola
Conductor	Gong	Tenorhorn	Violin
Cornet	Harp		

ⓘ DID YOU KNOW?

The oboe takes its name from the French word hautbois – which literally means "high wood"!

50

All the numbers from 1 to 16 fit into the gaps in this number square. Given the totals at the end of each row and column, can you complete the square with the missing numbers?

1 2 ~~3~~ 4 ~~5~~ 6 ~~7~~ 8 9 10 ~~11~~ 12 13 14 ~~15~~

	+	9	+		+	5	**31**
+		+		+		+	
	+		+		+	3	**38**
+		+		+		+	
14	+	7	+		+	15	**42**
+		+		+		+	
11	+	8	+		+		**25**
36		**37**		**38**		**25**	

51

The answers to these 11 questions all have something in common. Can you work out what that is for an extra bonus point?

1. How is the superhero Tony Stark better known?

2. What was the name of the Lone Ranger's horse?

3. The tuba and euphonium belong to what family of musical instruments?

4. What is the closest planet to the sun?

5. Which character in the *Wizard of Oz* wanted a heart?

6. What is a coin worth 5 cents known as in the United States?

7. What classic Charles Dickens novel features the characters Clara Peggotty and Wilkins Micawber?

8. Despite being made of graphite, what is the writing filament of a pencil called?

9. What is the famous one-mile-long red bridge that spans San Francisco Bay in California known as?

10. What metal percussion instrument, originally from the Carribean island of Trinidad, is also known as a pan drum?

11. What medal is awarded to an athlete who finishes in third place in the Olympic Games?

12. What connects all the previous answers?

52

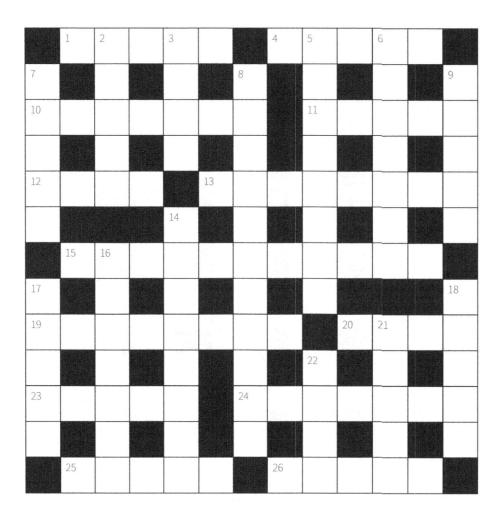

Across

1. Not moving (5)
4. Coastal sandy area (5)
10. A thousand thousands (6)
11. Stun (5)
12. Protracted (4)
13. Hot and humid (8)
15. Animated cat and mouse duo (3, 3, 5)
19. Came back (8)
20. Long-necked waterbird (4)
23. Forbidden, not to be spoken of (5)
24. Idea, concept (7)
25. The print media (5)
26. Turn red with effort or heat (5)

Down

2. Bird of prey's claw (5)
3. Animal's den (4)
5. Specimens, case studies (8)
6. *Canterbury Tales* author (7)
7. Little (5)
8. Things listed in a recipe (11)
9. Vends, exchanges for money (5)
14. Fierce fighters (8)
16. Halloween's month (7)
17. Wooden cargo box (5)
18. Individual items (5)
21. Salaries (5)
22. Area of water for swimming (4)

53

Place the answers to these questions letter by letter into the boxes, then move the letters into their corresponding boxes in the coded message at the bottom of the page to reveal a famous Bible verse.

1. What is the surname of Jodie, who took over the role of *Doctor Who* in 2017?

    1 __ 2 __ 3 __ 4 __ 5 __ 6 __ 7 __ 8 __ 9 __

2. Titan is a moon of what planet?

    10 __ 11 __ 12 __ 13 __ 14 __ 15 __

3. Which American singer's hits include "Positions" and "Thank U, Next"?

    16 __ 17 __ 18 __ 19 __ 20 __ 21 __ 22 __ 23 __ 24 __ 25 __

    26 __ 27 __

4. What name is given to a word that sounds the same as another, but is spelled differently—like blue and blew?

    28 __ 29 __ 30 __ 31 __ 32 __ 33 __ 34 __ 35 __ 36 __

5. In what country are the Parthenon and the Acropolis?

    37 __ 38 __ 39 __ 40 __ 41 __ 42 __

6. What is the highest prime number below 20?

    43 __ 44 __ 45 __ 46 __ 47 __ 48 __ 49 __ 50 __

7. What name is given to a noticeably dark region on the surface of the sun?

    51 __ 52 __ 53 __ 54 __ 55 __ 56 __ 57 __

8. Complete this line from the famous nursery rhyme, "And ___ ran away with the spoon".

    58 __ 59 __ 60 __   61 __ 62 __ 63 __ 64 __

9. Proverbially, what are you said to "jump on" when you join in with a trend?

    65 __ 66 __ 67 __ 68 __ 69 __ 70 __ 71 __ 72 __ 73 __

10. What common medical complain can be cluster, sinus, tension, or migraine?

74 __ 75 __ 76 __ 77 __ 78 __ 79 __ 80 __ 81 __

11. What name links the sportsman Beckham and broadcaster Attenborough?

82 __ 83 __ 84 __ 85 __ 86 __

12. What soft white crumbly cheese is served in a traditional Greek salad?

87 __ 88 __ 89 __ 90 __

"3 __ 50 __   57 __ 74 __ 36 __

65 __ 39 __ 22 __ 18 __ 20 __ 15 __ 85 __ 67 __ 71 __,

37 __ 29 __ 61 __   41 __ 23 __ E6 __ T46 __ 26 __

12 __ 33 __ E   2 __ 48 __ 83 __ V27 __ N   70 __ 45 __ D

T28 __ E   81 __ 19 __ 14 __ 47 __ H .

16 __ 53 __ D   T59 __ 42 __   88 __ 76 __ 9 __ T64

W11 __ 51 __   1 __ 44 __ 58 __ 80 __ 56 __ 52 __ 5 __

87 __ O38 __ 30 __,   66 __ 73 __ D

84 __ 31 __ 62 __ 82 ;   21 __ 25 __ 86 __

68 __ 78 __ 17 __ 7 __ 35 __ 60 __ 63 __ 10 __

69 __ 90 __ 54 __   13 __ 55 __ 72 __ 43 __

4 __ H49 __   F24 __ 79 __ 75 __

34 __ F   89 __ H40 __ 77 __ 8 __ E32 __ ."

54

Place the answers to the clues in the corresponding rows to spell out the name of a country reading downward in the shaded column.

1. Up to the point at which

2. The daughter of your brother or sister

3. Goa and Agra are cities in this country

4. Number of books in a trilogy

5. Very keen or enthusiastic

6. Famous biblical king

7. Oven; anagram of VOTES

8. In that place; not here

9. Once more

10. Coil, screw into a spiral

11. Large bird of prey that can be bald or golden, for example

12. Word that can mean both not tall and not long

13. Pungent vegetable that can make you cry!

14. Not true

15. A mixture of metals

16. Engine

17. African country famous for its pharaohs

18. Like the Amazon, the Danube, or the Ganges, for example

19. Alphabetical guide at the back of a book

20. Game that ends in a checkmate

21. Fictional character who explored Wonderland

#					
1					L
2				C	
3					A
4		H			
5		A			
6		A			
7				V	
8		H		R	
9		G			
10			I		
11					E
12			O		
13				O	
14		A			
15			L		
16			T		
17					T
18		I			
19				X	
20		H			S
21					E

55

Ghosts, ghouls, monsters, and mythical creatures are the theme of this crisscross puzzle. Can you find homes for all these legendary beings in the grid below?

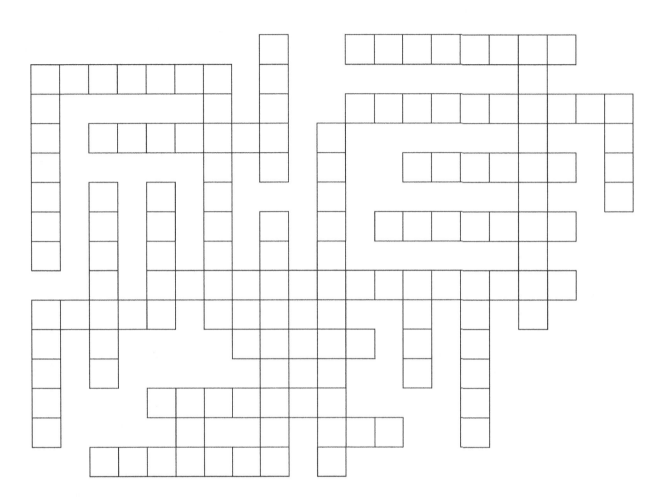

3 letters
Elf
Imp

4 letters
Ogre
Yeti

5 letters
Ghost
Ghoul
Giant
Pixie
Troll

6 letters
Dragon
Sphinx

7 letters
Bigfoot
Centaur
Cyclops
Gytrash
Pegasus
Unicorn
Vampire

8 letters
Basilisk

9 letters
Manticore
Sasquatch

10 letters
Sea monster
Tooth Fairy

12 letters
Shapeshifter

15 letters
Loch Ness Monster

56

Place the answers to the clues in the corresponding rows to spell out the name of a country reading downward in the shaded column.

A

1. __ __ — I think, therefore I __

2. __ __ __ — You'd find one in an atlas!

3. __ __ __ M — Inside of the hand

4. __ __ __ __ S — Lights

5. __ __ M __ __ __ — Taster; try a little bit of

6. __ M __ __ __ S — Pierces, stabs all the way through

7. __ __ S __ __ __ __ — Lose

57

Can you decode this cryptogram to spell out a famous piece of proverbial advice?

F R I I O N Q P W Y N U X O F X R I D

F R I L V N B

__ __E EAR__ __ __ __R__ __A__ __ __E__

__ __E __ __RM

58

Across

1. Some

7. In that place

8. Organ of hearing

9. Stag

11. Cease

13. Neither

14. Say, put into words

16. Alterations

Down

2. The day before

3. Flat; equal

4. Make aware

5. Pupil

6. Ready, arrange

10. Soil

12. Rotate

15. Knot

59

60

You'll have to study this grid carefully…the names of 24 different "ologies" and fiends of study are hidden in the wordsearch below!

```
Y O A I E O O L O G Y A Y O G
G N Y S A C Z Y S G Y R G R E
O C G G T O O O G Y C O N O
L O O S O R C L O G W H L I L
O L L L B I O L O G Y E O T O
R O O O O T O L A G O O N H G
D G P L U C O N O Y Y L H O Y
Y Y O A Y F T L W G W O C L G
H G T M U H N C L G Y G E O O
Y G O L O N A P M A C Y T G L
Y G O L O P O R H T N A O Y O
Y G O L O M Y T E F Z Y I D M
L G P S Y C H O L O G Y B W S
Y D I A L E C T O L O G Y F O
N U M E R O L O G Y Q D C G C
```

Anthology	Biology	Ecology	Numerology	Sociology
Anthropology	Biotechnology	Etymology	Oncology	Topology
Archeology	Campanology	Geology	Oology	
Astrology	Cosmology	Hydrology	Ornithology	Ufology
Autology	Dialectology	Mycology	Psychology	Zoology

ⓘ DID YOU KNOW?

Oology listed here is the scientific study of birds' eggs.

61

Fill the answers to the clues into the corresponding rows on the left, and a well known phrase will appear reading downward in the shaded column.

1. Mount Kilimanjaro is this continent's highest mountain

2. First name of filmmaker Spielberg

3. Family member the word "paternal" relates to

4. Summer month named after a Roman emperor

5. Burrowing rodent that lives in a warren

6. Charles Dickens or Philip Pullman, for example

7. Place of education

8. Rafael Nadal's sport

9. If breadth is horizontal, then __ is vertical

10. Mistakes, slipups

11. Exertion, energy used up

12. Like bananas, lemons, or canaries, for example

13. Winne the Pooh's glum donkey friend

14. Manmade waterways used by boats

15. At all times, on every occasion

16. Figure, digit

17. Oscar-winning actress Bullock

18. Continent on which the river Rhine is found

19. Provide more than expected; go beyond usual limits

#						
1						
2				V		
3						R
4		U				
5				B		
6			T			
7				O		
8						S
9			I			
10			R		R	
11		F	F			
12						W
13				O		
14			N		L	
15		L	W			
16				B		
17						
18		U				
19		X	C			

ⓘ DID YOU KNOW?

*The actress in **QUESTION 17** here is fluent in German, and holds dual German and American citizenship. Her mother, Helga, was an opera singer and vocal coach from Germany!*

62

Across

1. Old valuable object (7)

5. Excellent (5)

8. Nominate for a job or role (7)

9. Parts of a house (5)

10. Cairo's country (5)

11. Redraft (7)

12. Backstreets (6)

14. Take on board (6)

17. People lacking courage (7)

19. Arrive at; touch (5)

22. Explode like a volcano (5)

23. Reuses a contains (7)

24. Canvas bags (5)

25. Lack of sound (7)

Down

1. Conscious of (5)

2. Slightly drunk (5)

3. Gently, inaudibly (7)

4. Whole, complete (6)

5. Drinking tube (5)

6. Oath (7)

7. Admiration; regard for someone (7)

12. Very old(7)

13. Legal proceedings (7)

15. With great attention (7)

16. Famous Egyptian god (6)

18. Scores, critiques (5)

20. Putting everything into a bet (3-2)

21. Speed (5)

63

All the answers in this quiz end in the same two letters. Once you know what those are, you might be able to use them to figure out some of the tougher questions…

1. Who was the legendary captain of the Argonauts in Greek mythology?

2. What is the large pot in which a witch brews her potions called?

3. Which Oscar-winning actress played Nanny McPhee on the big screen?

4. Which American president resigned as a result of the Watergate scandal?

5. Which famous English poet died of a fever while in Greece in 1824?

6. How is the American buffalo better known?

7. What name is given to the punctuation mark comprising two dots arranged one on top of the other, (:) ?

8. What west African country has a flag of green, red, and yellow vertical stripes, in the middle of which is a single yellow star?

9. What manmade fabric is popularly (though wrongly!) claimed to take its name from the fact that it was invented by two teams of scientists, one from New York and the other from London?

10. What wild big cat as a thick covering of hair around its head called a mane?

64

All the five-letter words below are missing one of their letters. Fill in the gaps to spell out a 12-letter word reading down the middle.

1. C __ OOK
2. NIC __ R
3. __ IGHT
4. W __ TER
5. MO __ OR
6. MED __ C

7. SP __ OK
8. __ IGHT
9. __ IGHT
10. __ OTEL
11. SL __ NK
12. PA __ ER

65

There are some great words in this crisscross puzzle—but you'd not want to be called any of them!

4 letters
Foul
Sour

5 letters
Catty
Crude
Lying
Nasty
Pesky

6 letters
Boring
Smarmy

7 letters
Irksome

8 letters
Annoying
Cheating
Churlish
Spiteful
Terrible

9 letters
Invidious
Obstinate
Pig-headed

10 letters
Malevolent
Unfriendly
Ungenerous
Unpleasant
Vindictive

11 letters
Bad-tempered
Belligerent
Ill-mannered
Infuriating
Sycophantic
Troublesome

12 letters
Mean-spirited
Potty-mouthed

66

This is a mega word pyramid! Starting from a single letter, you'll have to add **OR** remove a letter from the previous answer to answer all the clues. Can you get all the way from **A** to **B** to **C** to **D**?

A

1.	__ __	Commercial
2.	__ __ __	Terrible
3.	__ __ __ **D**	Pop group, ensemble
4.	**B** __ __ __ __	Style, make
5.	__ __ __ __ **D** __	Hollywood legend Marlon
6.	**B** __ __ __ __	Enter a ship
7.	__ __ __ **D**	Shakespeare, for instance
8.	**B** __ __	Tavern, inn
9.	__ __	Barium

B

10.	__ __	Russian river
11.	__ **O** __	Sound of a fright
12.	__ __ __ **R**	Ill-mannered person
13.	__ __ **R** __ __	Chemical element no. 5
14.	__ __ __ __ __ __	Unpredictable horse ridden in a rodeo
15.	__ **R O** __ __	Sing like a 1950s star
16.	__ __ __ __	Maize
17.	__ __ __	Deception
18.	__ __	Cartoon Network

C

19. ___ ___   Prefix meaning joint or mutual

20. ___ ___ ___   Atlantic fish popular in cookery

21. ___ ___ ___ **D**   Thick nerve of the spinal column

22. ___ ___ ___ ___ **D**   Large group of people

23. ___ ___ ___ ___ ___ **D**   Scaredy-cat

24. ___ **R** ___ ___ ___   *Harry Potter's* Mr Malfoy

25. ___ ___ ___ ___   Thick paper

26. ___ ___ **D**   Bounder, rogue

27. ___ ___   Father

D

67

All the words in this fiendish wordsearch contain eight letters!

Addition	Magazine
Argument	Midnight
Category	Patience
Contract	Platform
Currency	Priority
Database	Property
Decision	Quantity
Delivery	Resource
Elevator	Security
Employee	Shopping
Employer	Stranger
Hospital	Sympathy
Industry	Teaching

```
T M A G A Z I N E G Y S D Q O
D E C I S I O N V K G Y E U Y
C A T E G O R Y D N H M L A T
R E Y O L P M E I U N P I N I
T M I D N I G H T V S A V T R
R E S O U R C E P O C T E I O
L P D Y A A M C P U M H R T I
R A A E E T O S R E P Y Y Y R
E T T T L N M R O F T A L P P
G I A I T E E M P L O Y E E R
N E B R P N V S E C U R I T Y
A N A H C S W A R G U M E N T
R C S Y W N O I T I D D A M W
T E E M I X Q H Y O U O R N W
S G N I P P O H S E R E V K H
```

68

Place the answers to the following questions, letter by letter, into the numbered boxes. Then move the letters into the corresponding boxes in the coded message at the bottom of the page to reveal a famous quote from the *Harry Potter* stories.

1. What species of big cat is native to the Amazon rainforest?

1 __ 2 __ 3 __ 4 __ 5 __ 6 __

2. What ant-like insects are known for the damage they can cause to timbers?

7 __ 8 __ 9 __ 10 __ 11 __ 12 __ 13 __ 14 __

3. By what name is a cockerel also known?

15 __ 16 __ 17 __ 18 __ 19 __ 20 __ 21 __

4. What is the female equivalent of an emperor?

22 __ 23 __ 24 __ 25 __ 26 __ 27 __ 28 __

5. In grammar, what is a word that describes how an action takes place called?

29 __ 30 __ 31 __ 32 __ 33 __ 34 __

6. In the *Peanuts* comic strips, what is Charlie Brown's dog called?

35 __ 36 __ 37 __ 38 __ 39 __ 40 __

7. What does the A stand for in the netball positions WA and GA?

41 __ 42 __ 43 __ 44 __ 45 __ 46 __

8. What is the meat of a fully-grown sheep known as?

47 __ 48 __ 49 __ 50 __ 51 __ 52 __

9. What is a structured, searchable set of computer information known as?

53 __ 54 __ 55 __ 55 __ 56 __ 57__ 58 __ 59 __ 60 __

10. What bodily hormone regulates the amount of glucose in the blood?

61 __ 62 __ 63 __ 64 __ 65 __ 66 __ 67 __

11. Popular in skiing resorts, what name is given to a pot of melted cheese into which skewered meats, vegetables, and bread can be dipped?

68 __ 69 __ 70 __ 71 __ 72 __ 73 __

12. What is the name of the light skirt worn by a ballerina?

74 __ 75 __ 76 __ 77 __

" 61 __ 7 __   12 __ 29 __ 46 __ 22 __ 35 __   2 __

3 __ 9 __ 20 __ 58 __ 43 __   53 __ 13 __ 44 __ 65 __

O 68 __   57 __ 21 __ 41 __ 31 __ 73 __ 25 __ 40 __

42 __ 37 __   59 __ 19 __ 54 __ 62 __ 30 __   75 __ 39 __

74 __ 38 __   16 __ 72 __ 6 __

32 __ 36 __ 60 __ 23 __ 11 __ 8 __ 18 __ ,   34 __ 64 __ 55 __

1 __ U 27 __ T   5 __ 63 __   10 __ 77 __ 45 __ H

T 17 __   28 __ 76 __ 56 __ 67 __ 71 __   4 __ 24 __   TO

69 __ U 33 __   F 15 __ 66 __ 26 __ 70 __ D 14 __ . "

69

To solve this anagram acrostic, you must unjumble the words on the right and place them in the corresponding spaces in the grid on the left. When you're done, the name of a day in the calendar will read down the shaded column!

1. Rec hill
2. I hold ya
3. Corders
4. Land sis
5. Jet cubs
6. Say duet
7. Gases me
8. I parrot
9. Plaices
10. Max peel
11. Love tag
12. Shingle

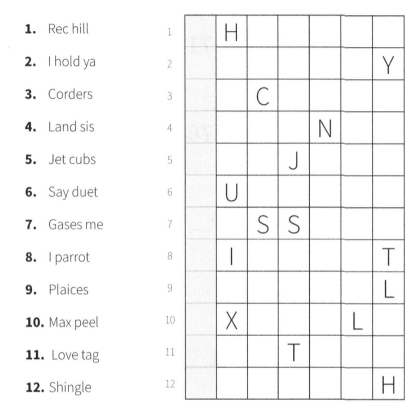

70

Here are all the answers to this crossword—with a twist! They've all been jumbled up. Can you unscramble each clue and restore the crossword to its former glory?

Across

1. China
4. Tug
6. Sue
7. Stale
8. Curbs
9. Caned
13. Lamer
14. God
15. Hes
16. Groan

Down

1. Encradles
2. Raja
3. Stun
4. Rage
5. Brainstem
10. Dune
11. Gore
12. Nags

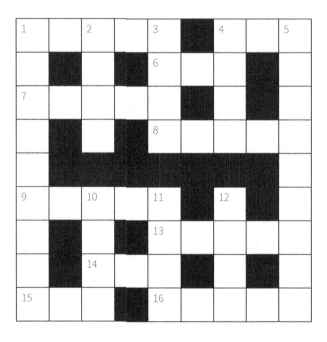

71

Can you find all of these mobile phone apps in the grid below?

```
E T M E S S E N G E R A W S S
R E W S C M P B Y A R P E L S
O L D I E T A O A E X P A I A
T L Z K T N U P D Y K L T A P
S A E K T T U A S T O E H M M
P W T L U A E T S Z T M E E O
P L R B G R H R I O K U R G C
A L E E E O F C A O I S N C W
F A C E B O O K P M T I G H B
Y F I T O P S G W A L C A N B
M A R G E L E T F O N T M E R
G N I K N A B M U V S S E W A
C A M E R A H D S A V I S S V
P H O N E Y A L P E L G O O G
M A Z A H S Z P T I C K E T S
```

Apple music	Ebay	Itunes	Snapchat	Wallet
Appstore	Emails	Maps	Spotify	Weather
Banking	Ereader	Messenger	Telegram	Whatsapp
Camera	Facebook	News	Tickets	
Compass	Games	Phone	Tiktok	Youtube
Duolingo	Google play	Shazam	Twitter	Zoom

72

SPOT THE 12 DIFFERENCES

1	17	21	15	5	17	8		8	14	22	15	1
3		17		14		14		5		14		22
20	14	2	15	9		22	9	14	26	3	6	15
15		19		15		14		1		2		3
9	15	15	18	1		2	15 E	6 T	8 W	17 O	9	19
	23					12		4				15
3	1	1	14	1	6		19	15	15	22	15	9
10				25		20				4		
10	5	3	21	7	15	9		8	5	3	4	15
25		10		24		15		9		6		13
1	11	25	15	15	16	15		17	22	15	9	3
15		6		10		4		2		3		10
1	22	15	2	6		23	17	12	5	25	9	6

A B C D E F G H I J K L M N O P Q R S T U V W X Y Z

1	2	3	4	5	6	7	8	9	10	11	12	13
14	15	16	17	18	19	20	21	22	23	24	25	26

74

Decode this cryptogram to spell out a famous saying.

ZJU JKUPLV FUP'Z OSEH S
KQLRZ

__ W __   W __ __ __ GS   __ __ __ '__   __ __ __ E   __
__ __ G __ __

75

S

1. __ __   Cool __ a cucumber

2. __ __ __ __   Ocean

3. __ __ A __   Join in a garment

4. __ A __ __ __   Men

5. __ __ A __ __ S   Accuses of doing something bad

6. __ __ __ B __ __ S   Small glass balls for playing games

7. __ __ A __ B __ __ S   Climbs over awkwardly

7. S __ __ __ __ B __ __ __   Method of cooking eggs

76

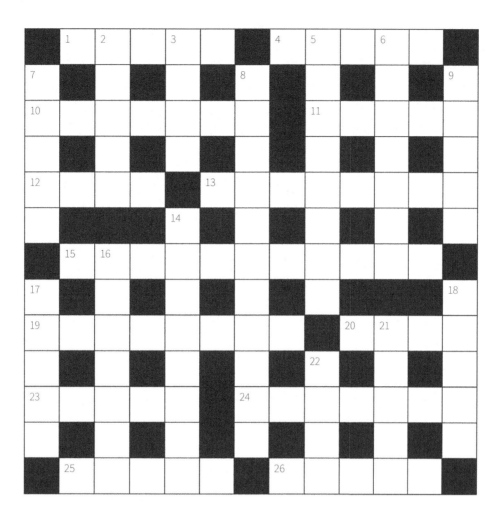

Across

1. Alphabetical list at the back of a book (5)

4. Caustic liquids (5)

10. Bags taken on holiday (7)

11. Stony (5)

12. Performs on stage (4)

13. Power, might (8)

15. Exceptionally wonderful (11)

19. Drugstore (8)

20. Horseback ballsport (4)

23. Incompetent (5)

24. Tutor (7)

25. Unsophisticated; boorish (5)

26. Liner, transport ship (5)

Down

2. Period of darkness (5)

3. School test (4)

5. National money unit (8)

6. Ten-sided shape (7)

7. Scour (5)

8. Formal document of qualifications (11)

9. Legends (5)

14. Enlivened (8)

16. Keen beginner (7)

17. Divide, break up (5)

18. Word of apology (5)

21. Alternative option (5)

22. Naked (4)

77

Can you find a home for all these ball games in the grid below?

4 letters

Golf

Polo

Pool

5 letters

Bandy

Bocce

Bowls

Carom

Fives

Rugby

6 letters

Boules

Pelota

Soccer

Squash

Tennis

7 letters

Bowling

Cricket

Croquet

Hurling

Jai alai

Netball

Pinball

Snooker

8 letters

Handball

Korfball

Lacrosse

Petanque

Rounders

Slamball

Softball

9 letters

Bagatelle

Billiards

Quidditch

11 letters

Aussie rules

Field hockey

Knuckleball

Racquetball

16 letters

American football

Pop superstar Taylor Swift is the subject of this wordsearch. How many of her hit singles and albums can you find in the grid below?

All you had to do /
Was stay

August

Bad blood

Blank space

Cardigan

Delicate

Dress

Evermore

Folklore

Gorgeous

I knew you /
Were trouble

Look what you /
Made me do

Lover

Love story

Out of the woods

Style

The man

Wildest / Dreams

Willow

You belong /
With me

```
I T S U O E G R O G Z F O M M M
K L S W L R R C D R C D S A E M
N O S E W O A O L S O Y M D E R
E V R S D R O O L T S O A E O
W E V I D L V K D K F E E M M
Y R X I B E I A W W L T R E R
O I G D S W H W N H I O D D E
U A A T S U G U A M A T F O V
N B O T O T H E M A N T H B E
G R L Y C X W A S S T A Y M O
Y E L B U O R T E R E W T O E
B L A N K S P A C E S L I Z U
A Y O U B E L O N G N N Y V S
S D O O W E H T F O T U O T Z
D E L I C A T E W O L L I W S
```

ⓘ DID YOU KNOW?

When she won in 2020 with her surprise lockdown album folklore, Taylor Swift became the first and only female solo artist to win the Grammy Award for Album of The Year three times! She had already won the award for Fearless in 2009, and 1989 in 2015.

79

The same three letters can be added onto the end of all eight of these words. What are they—and what are the new words?

ANY   __ __ __   KNOW   __ __ __

CHATS   __ __ __   ROADS   __ __ __

DOGS   __ __ __   SIDES   __ __ __

GAMES   __ __ __   SOME   __ __ __

80

Each of the answers to these 20 questions begins with a different letter of the alphabet. Once you've answered them all, rearrange the remaining six unused letters to spell out the name of a European city.

A B C D E F G H I J K L M N O P Q R S T U V W X Y Z

1. Hokkaido and Honshu are islands in what country?
2. A vixen is a female of what animal?
3. In what month is Fool's Day celebrated?
4. Justin Trudeau because prime minister of what country in 2015?
5. Who was the king of the gods in Greek mythology?
6. What is the surname of the infamously miserly Dickens character Ebenezer?
7. What was the name of Queen Elizabeth II's father?
8. The Savoy in London and The Plaza in New York are what kind of business?
9. What is the rising agent of bread?
10. What pair of bodily organs are located on either side of the lower back?
11. What team sport has versions played on horseback and in a swimming pool?
12. What Middle Eastern nation hosted the 2022 FIFA World Cup?
13. What percussion instrument has a name meaning "wooden sound" in Greek?
14. What was the name of US president George Washington's wife?
15. What planet of the solar system lies between Saturn and Neptune?
16. "Food, Glorious Food" is a song from what stage musical?
17. 15, 30, 40, deuce, and advantage are scores used in what sport?
18. What was the middle initial of US president George Bush, Jr.?
19. What infamous conflict lasted from 1955-1975?
20. According to the title of a classic 1971 James Bond film, what *Are Forever*?

BONUS ANSWER: _____

HARD

Let's make things a little tougher!

81

Across

1. Stretchy (7)

5. Lantern (5)

8. Abide by the rules (7)

9. Blacksmith's block (5)

10. Hairdresser's workplace (5)

11. Return to former glory (7)

12. Very scary (13)

16. Mock, spoof (7)

18. Punctuation mark (5)

20. Feel (5)

21. Pressing clothes (7)

22. Stairs (5)

23. Cricket teams (7)

Down

1. Reasons (7)

2. Cancel (5)

3. Defeat (7)

4. Very thorough (13)

5. Sides, groups (5)

6. Pasta parcels (7)

7. Split in two (5)

13. Of enormous size (7)

14. Milk sugar (7)

15. Homesteads, ranches (7)

16. Misplaces (5)

17. Unlocks (5)

19. Corn (5)

82

	8		19		7		25		22		5	
19	6	26	6	17	6		6	22 C	10 H	3 O	6 E	15
	17		14		6		26		13		13	
11	16	14	4		24	16	12	2	14	22	2	9
			6		14		19		17		3	
1	6	6	15	14	17	21		14	19	19	16	6
	20				21		22				19	
19	22	13	2	6		22	3	18	12	3	9	19
	10		13		19		8		26			
10	13	26	15	19	10	14	24		13	26	8	19
	17		15		13		2		17		13	
13	21	26	6	6	15		6	20	22	6	24	23
	6		26		9		20		10		19	

A B C D E F G H I J K L M N O P Q R S T U V W X Y Z

1	2	3	4	5	6	7	8	9	10	11	12	13
14	15	16	17	18	19	20	21	22	23	24	25	26

Place the answers to the clues on the right into the corresponding rows in the grid on the left, and the name of a famous London tourist attraction will be spelled out in the shaded column.

1. In what European country are the cities of Antwerp and Louvain?
2. In what South American nation was the very first FIFA World Cup held in 1930?
3. In Greek mythology, what name is given to a one-eyed giant?
4. What term for singing to a backing track derives from the Japanese for "empty orchestra"?
5. Lines that link places with the same air pressure on a weather map are called what?
6. Which famous horseshoe waterfalls straddles the border between the US and Canada?
7. What is the surname of Paul, the famous French Post-Impressionist artist known for his paintings of life in Polynesia?
8. What famous US university is located in Cambridge, Massachusetts?
9. What kind of building is Orly in Paris, or Schiphol in Amsterdam?
10. What is the surname of the English playwright and poet Christopher—a contemporary of Shakespeare who was stabbed to death in a fight in a London tavern in 1593?
11. What is the surname of Sarah, the actress who starred in nine out of the first ten series of *American Horror Story*?
12. What tiny European country is located high in the Pyrenees mountains between France and Spain?
13. Which US president was assassinated on 15 April 1865?
14. In what US state is the Grand Canyon?
15. How are knives, forks, spoons, and other eating implements collectively known?
16. The official languages of Kenya are Swahili and which other?

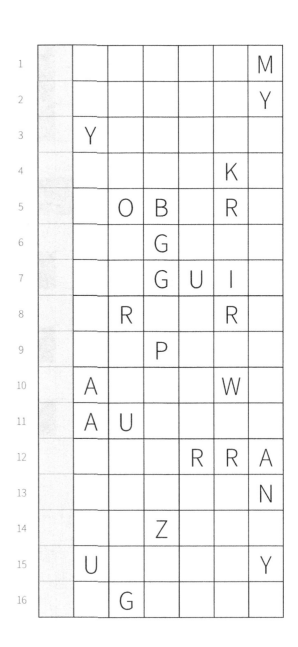

84

3 letters
Ely

4 letters
Bath
York

5 letters
Derby
Derry
Perth
Ripon
Wells

6 letters
Armagh
Oxford

7 letters
Belfast
Bristol
Glasgow
Lisburn
Salford
Swansea

8 letters
Aberdeen
Hereford
Plymouth
St Albans
St David's

9 letters
Cambridge
Inverness
Leicester
Wakefield

10 letters
Canterbury

12 letters
Brighton Hove
Stoke-on-Trent

85

Can you decipher this cryptogram to spell out a well-known proverb?

Y M N   B V V Z N   F N T N J   D B Z Z K   D B J

D J P O   Y M N   Y J N N

_ _ E _ _ _ _ E _ E _ E _ F_ _ _ _ F_ _

F_ _ _ _ _ E _ _ EE

86

1. What time is 0000 on a 24-hour clock?
2. If a carnivore eats meat, and a herbivore eats plants, what name is given to a creature that eats all foods?
3. What boxing division comes between lightweight and bantamweight?
4. Who famously interviewed Prince Harry and Meghan Markle on television in 2021?
5. What tree produces conkers?
6. In what country is the ancient city of Machu Picchu?
7. What chess piece can only move diagonally?
8. What kind of foodstuff are parmesan and halloumi?
9. How many strings does a cello have?
10. Who wrote the classic English novel *Jane Eyre*?
11. Where were the 2012 Olympic Games held?
12. The mysterious Bermuda Triangle is a region of which ocean?
13. What device has a lens, viewfinder, shutter, and flash?
14. In what decade of the 20th century did Elizabeth II become queen?
15. What is the past tense form of the verb bring?
16. What can be gloss, emulsion, oil, or poster?
17. In which country was Mozart born?
18. Anubis was a god in which ancient mythology?
19. The Pantanal is a vast wetland region of which South American river?
20. What kind of geographical feature is the Matterhorn?

87

We're heading into the kitchen for this wordsearch. How many of these cooking appliances and utensils can you find in the grid below?

```
R E T A R G R G R X B F G L C C Q H
T L A D L E L E T R L O R W A R B S
Q E W U K A N R E S E N I O S O R I
C O K O S E J H E Z N D L B T C O D
K R O S P M S D U Z D U L T I K O R
S C E O A A P R O N E E L I R P M E
A S N A W B C T E Y R E A U O O K T
U A B H M S D A E K O V R R N T O T
C S S F F E I A S P A L R F P E O U
E I K R O F R F E S D M E G A L B B
D K N I S B L N T R E E E W N B K K
E G G T I M E R V E B R C E O A O N
R E D N I R G A X N R K O A F T O I
C O O K I E C U T T E R F L N F C F
D R A O B P U C K E T T L E E T O E
L W O B G K Y K C A R H S I D O E C
S K C I T S P O H C G R I D D L E R
C A R A F E C U T T I N G B O A R D
```

Apron	Canopener	Cookiecutter	Dishwasher	Glasses	Ladle
Beater	Carafe	Creamer	Eggtimer	Grater	Sauce
Blender	Casserole	Crockpot	Fondue	Griddle	Sifter
Bottleopener	Castironpan	Cupboard	Food	Grill	Sink
Bowl	Chopsticks	Cuttingboard	Fork	Grinder	Table
Breadbasket	Coffeemaker	Decanter	Freezer	Kettle	Towel
Broom	Cookbook	Dishrack	Fruitbowl	Knife	Wok
Butterdish	Cooker				

88

SPOT THE 12 DIFFERENCES

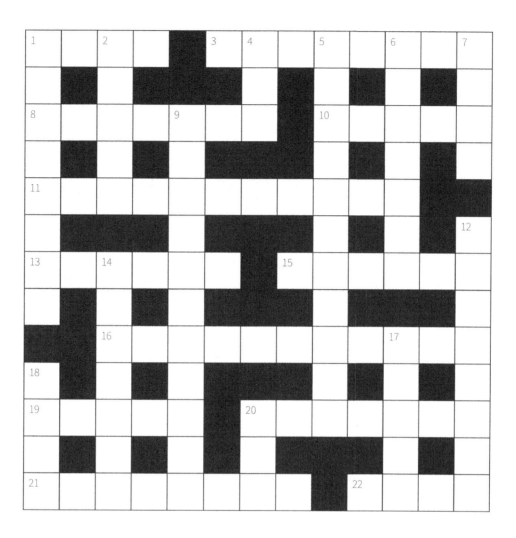

Across

1. Insects (4)

3. Travel document (8)

8. Outtake (7)

10. Adversary (5)

11. Understood, taken to mean (11)

13. Counting frame (6)

15. Plan, ploy (6)

16. People who help a criminal (11)

19. US state on the Canadian border (5)

21. Shorten a novel (7)

21. Examined data thoroughly (8)

22. Proof, correct text (4)

Down

1. Scriptural (7)

2. Apparition (5)

4. Gas that is breathed (3)

5. Extraordinarily good (11)

6. Still to be paid, like a bill (7)

7. Playthings (4)

9. Brief and to the point; cursory (11)

12. Most untidy (8)

14. Montgomery is its capital (7)

17. Ciphered, having its meaning hidden (5)

18. Grand female singer (4)

20. Beer (3)

90

Place the answers to the clues on the right into the corresponding rows in the grid on the left, and the name of a famous sports team will be spelled out downward in the shaded column.

1. Who played Willy Wonka in the original 1971 movie adaptation of *Charlie and the Chocolate Factory?* (4, 6)

2. What Taylor Swift album included the singles "Delicate", "…Ready For It?", and "Look What You Made Me Do"?

3. What popular novel by John Steinbeck features the character Cyrus Trask? (4,2,4)

4. Who was the 34th US president, who as a general in the US Army had overseen the Normandy Landings of the Second World War?

5. Which English city's sheriff was Robin Hood's adversary?

6. Dhaka is the capital of what Asian country?

7. In the Bible, who were the parents of Cain and Abel? (4,3,3)

8. What European country broke apart in 1991, making the constituent countries of Croatia, Slovenia, and Bosnia independent nations?

#	1	2	3	4	5	6	7	8	9	10
1		E			W					R
2			P					I		N
3		A		T		F		D		
4						H				
5				T	T		G			
6									S	H
7		D							V	
8			G							A
9			C				C		I	
10				X						A
11						F				A
12			N				R			S
13						Q				
14					O				R	R
15		T			E			N		

9. What 2013 movie starring Charlie Hunnam was about gigantic human-piloted robots battling enormous sea monsters from another dimension? (7,3)

10. What Ancient Egyptian city was famous for its lighthouse and its library?

11. In what US state is Silicon Valley?

12. What famous London train station is supposedly where the Hogwarts Express can be caught from Platform 9¾? (5,5,)

13. What geological event would be measured on a seismograph?

14. Who was the drummer in the Beatles? (5,5)

15. What is the name of the famous stone circle in southeast England, thought to have been built by ancient Druid priests more than 5,000 years ago?

91

Place the answers to the following questions letter by letter into the numbered boxes. Then move the letters into their corresponding boxes in the coded message below to reveal a famous theatrical quotation.

1. Which Dr Seuss story features characters called Thing One and Thing Two?

1 __ 2 __ 3 __ 4 __ 5 __ 6 __ 7 __ 8 __ 9 __ 10 __ 11 __ 12 __
13 __ 14 __

2. The islands of Borneo, Sumatra, and New Guinea are part of what country?

15 __ 16 __ 17 __ 18 __ 19 __ 20 __ 21 __ 22 __ 23 __

3. What surname links Hollywood actor brothers Liam and Chris?

24 __ 25 __ 26 __ 27 __ 28 __ 29 __ 30 __ 31 __ 32 __

4. How is All Hallows' Eve better known?

33 __ 34 __ 35 __ 36 __ 37 __ 38 __ 39 __ 40 __ 41 __

5. In what bodily organ is digestive bile stored after it is produced in the liver?

42 __ 43 __ 44 __ 45 __ 46 __ 47 __ 48 __ 49 __ 50 __ 51 __ 52 __

6. What brightly colored root vegetable is used to make borscht soup?

53 __ 54 __ 55 __ 56 __ 57 __ 58 __ 59 __ 60 __

7. What word can either mean a sound's loudness or a vessel's capacity?

61 __ 62 __ 63 __ 64 __ 65 __ 66 __

8. According to the proverb, what is said to "favour the brave"?

67 __ 68 __ 69 __ 70 __ 71 __ 72 __ 73 __

9. What name is given to a botanical garden especially devoted to trees?

74 __ 75 __ 76 __ 77 __ 78 __ 79 __ 80 __ 81 __ 82 __

10. What is the name of the ticking device a musician uses to keep strict time?

83 __ 84 __ 85 __ 86 __ 87 __ 88 __ 89 __ 90 __ 91 __

11. He, she, him, and her are examples of what kind of word?

92 __ 91 __ 92 __ 93 __ 94 __ 95 __ 96 __ 97 __ 98 __

"37 __   57 __ 62 __ 90 __ 3 __ 18 __ ,

52 __ 77 __ 82 __ 25 __ 58 __ ,

28 __ 2 __ 73 __ R 20 __ 67 __ 89 __ 86 __ 66 __

13 __ R 31 __   70 __ 12 __ O 64 __

75 __ 59 __ 26 __ 79 __ 87 __ ?   17 __ 84 __ 16 __ Y

85 __ 32 __ Y   F 74 __ 60 __ 10 __ E 78 __   22 __ 95 __ 50 __

93 __ 54 __ F 97 __ 21 __ 39 __   9 __ 24 __ Y

98 __ 5 __ 65 __ 91 __ ; 96 __ R   15 __ F   1 __ 33 __ 68 __ 71 __

W 7 __ 44 __ 80 __   72 __ O 6 __ ,   53 __ 11 __

76 __ U 56 __   27 __ 38 __ O 69 __ 8 __   83 __ Y

47 __ 29 __ 61 __ 51 __   34 __ 41 __ 49 __

22 __ ' 35 __ 45 __   19 __ 94 __

36 __ O 88 __ 42 __ 55 __ 30 __   46 __ E   43 __

4 __ 48 __ 92 __ 81 __ 63 __ 40 __ 14 __ . "

I

1. __ __ — Fashionable, stylish at the moment

2. __ __ __ — Score of zero

3. __ __ __ __ — African big cat

4. __ __ __ I __ — Process of accessing a private website

5. __ B __ __ __ __ — Hideous imp

6. B __ __ __ __ __ __ — Game in which you can score a strike or a spare

7. __ __ B __ __ __ __ __ — Jostling out of the way

93

Decode this cryptogram to spell out a famous saying and proverb.

Y PJAQFSC JM Y EVJAIYFX
UGHSI OSKGFI DGEV Y
IGFKHS IESB

__ __O__ __ __ __ __   O__ __ __HO__ __ __ __

__ __ __ __S __ __ __ __ __S __ __ __H __

S__ __ __ __ __ S__ __ __

94

All the questions in this quiz have two answers. Can you pick up both points?

1. Sweden has land borders with which two other Scandinavian countries?

2. Who were the US President and British Prime Minister in the year 2000?

3. How many squares are on a chess board—and how many playing pieces does a player start with at the beginning of a game?

4. What are the first and last letters on the top row of a standard computer keyboard?

5. Which oceans lie to the east and west of North America?

6. What do the Latin phrases ante meridiem and post meridiem denote?

7. Which two pop superstars duetted on the 2012 hit "Everything Has Changed"?

8. A vast asteroid belt lies between which two planets in our solar system?

9. What two letters are silent in the word asthma?

10. On what two continents are wild tapirs found?

95

How about this for a wordsearch challenge! The names of all 50 of the United States are hidden somewhere in the grid. Can you find them all?

Alabama	Hawaii	Massachusetts	New Mexico	South Dakota
Alaska	Idaho	Michigan	New York	Tennessee
Arizona	Illinois	Minnesota	North Carolina	Texas
Arkansas	Indiana	Mississippi	North Dakota	Utah
California	Iowa	Missouri	Ohio	Vermont
Colorado	Kansas	Montana	Oklahoma	Virginia
Connecticut	Kentucky	Nebraska	Oregon	Washington
Delaware	Louisiana	Nevada	Pennsylvania	West Virginia
Florida	Maine	New Hampshire	Rhode Island	Wisconsin
Georgia	Maryland	New Jersey	South Carolina	Wyoming

```
B M I S S O U R I A Q S I L L I N O I S
X Y G N O R T H C A R O L I N A L S C U
E J E Q K M S T T E S U H C A S S A M J
G X O J T I C H L R O B H E B R A T E O
L S R R C N Z B M N U T R E P K N M D K
O G G A B N C Z I T T I C O S O A A P T
U T I R F E L S E P H R K A M A B R A X
I E A K T S N T R S C M L R C T V Y I O
S X C A K O O Y P O A A E Y D O M L N K
I A W N C T M E H R V W G E K I A I L
A S C S I A A N A K O H E Z L A S N G A
N P I A F H I W Z R L E S W A D S D R H
A W F S W A A G R N I S T Y W H I U I O
E R Z E M I L G N O N M V O A T S Q V M
V I N D I A N A E R A I I M R U S H X A
N P O S I H H V V T B C R I E O I N U N
E N E W S W G Z A H M H G N E S P F F C
W O A N A Y X H D D A I I G K P P A O Q
M T F V N E A D A A K G N M I U I N Z C
E G A I L S L N S K S A I L W Y N S O O
X N I S H R Y A Z O A N A Q X E Z L D O
I I N J N E S L E T R K C W C K O B H T
C H R A F J O S V A B I A T C R G A R N
O S O L L W U I M A E X I N A B D N N O
G A F A O E T E K N C X D S I J A E G
T W I B R N A D T H U I O I P A M T W E R
R T L A I U H O A T G N A L T S S N Y R
Y V A M D N O H I O Q Q K F I V I O O O
C E C A A F T R E E S S E N N E T M R M
A N O Z I R A T H L H Y K C U T N E K Z
```

ⓘ DID YOU KNOW?

The last US state alphabetically, Wyoming, is also the last state in terms of population—it's home to just over 575,000 people, despite being almost 100,000 square miles in size!

96

SPOT THE 12 DIFFERENCES

97

5	26 W	16 F	10 U	4 L	4	12		7	10	9	24	19
23		17		17		14		10		5		11
14	5	23	4	12		4	11	19	2	11	21	3
5		9		5		4		2		22		1
19	25	10	4	4		14	15	11	20	14	21	2
		4				20		13				14
13	4	5	10	19	14		8	14	3	3	14	20
5				1		24				23		
24	4	5	2	14	5	10		13	1	5	11	23
2		3		4		8		23		20		14
5	23	23	11	15	5	4		14	6	10	5	4
11		14		14		11		5		5		5
21	14	14	20	19		13	17	9	24	4	14	18

A B C D E F G H I J K L M N O P Q R S T U V W X Y Z

1	2	3	4	5	6	7	8	9	10	11	12	13
14	15	16	17	18	19	20	21	22	23	24	25	26

98

Across

1. Chill (4)
7. Victor, winner (8)
9. Female parent (6)
10. Chore (6)
11. Multiplied by two (7)
13. Competitor (5)
15. Condition; subdivision of the USA (5)
16. Real (7)
18. Vocals, sounds of speech (6)
19. Responds to (6)
21. Extends, draws out (8)

Down

1. One-person performance (4)
2. In A to Z order (12)
3. Vivid red (7)
4. H2O (5)
5. Decorative liquid spray (8)
8. Especially (12)
12. Not inside (8)
14. Closest (7)
17. Manipulating; utilizing (5)
20. Implement (4)

99

Can you find all 30 of these 7-figure number codes in the grid below?

```
5  8  9  0  1  3  2  0  1  5  8  6  9  4  6
3  5  5  9  5  1  1  3  0  2  6  8  5  4  6
5  9  2  5  5  5  8  4  2  6  3  8  3  3  7
8  2  9  5  4  1  6  1  5  9  3  5  7  4  5
7  1  6  2  7  0  9  5  2  2  8  4  8  9  8
4  0  3  0  8  2  6  9  6  1  0  9  9  3  9
0  6  5  1  6  5  0  7  5  9  8  6  2  0  3
2  5  1  4  2  5  3  1  3  5  2  4  9  9  9
1  4  5  5  6  5  0  0  6  5  8  3  3  1  6
4  7  5  8  8  5  2  2  5  3  1  4  0  4  9
5  0  4  9  9  8  0  4  1  8  5  2  1  1  1
9  8  7  6  5  3  9  4  3  5  1  7  5  2  8
9  2  8  3  6  2  1  4  1  9  9  9  9  5  1
6  3  2  0  6  2  1  4  5  0  0  8  7  1  8
4  9  6  3  3  5  4  2  2  0  3  2  3  0  2
```

1554782	3665986	7338362
1554786	5225314	7623854
1593574	5358740	8005412
1806405	5555201	8362141
2032302	5584263	8592106
3026589	5971024	9141251
3026895	6547082	9529635
3201586	6985410	9633542

100

Each of the answers to these questions begin and end with the same letter. Once you've solved them all, each question's letter, when read in order, will spell out the name of a capital city. Work that out for a bonus point!

1. How are circles drawn inside one another around the same midpoint known?

2. Iago and Desdemona are characters in which Shakespeare tragedy?

3. What was the name of Elizabeth II's husband, who died in 2021?

4. On which continent are the Loire, Tagus, and Po rivers found?

5. What colorless, odorless gas has the atomic number 7?

6. In what region of London is the famous Apollo Theatre located?

7. What field of math takes its name from the Arabic word for resetting bones?

8. Which famous environmental campaigner was born in Stockholm in 2003?

9. In the Bible, whom did God create from a rib bone?

10. Which US president had the first names Richard Milhous?

BONUS ANSWER: _____

101

This is another mega word pyramid! Starting from a single letter, you'll have to add OR remove a letter from the previous answer to answer all of the clues. Can you get all the way from B to A and back to B?

B

#		Clue
1.	__ __	Stomach muscle
2.	__ __ __	Nocturnal dark mammal
3.	__ __ __ __	2nd Greek letter
4.	B __ __ __ __	Wild animal
5.	__ __ __ __ __ T	Not present
6.	__ __ T __ __ __ __	Cricketers
7.	__ __ __ __ __ __ __ T	Cellar
8.	__ __ __ __ __ __ T	Most miserly or unpleasant
9.	__ E __ __ __ __	Sailors
10.	__ __ __ E __	Titles
11.	__ __ __ __	Identical
12.	__ __ __ __	First name of Oscar-winning actor Rockwell
13.	__ __	Like, by way of

A

#		Clue
14.	__ __	@
15.	__ __ __	Consumed
16.	__ __ __ __	Drop from the eye
17.	__ A __ __ __	Critiqued, scored
18.	__ __ __ A __ T	Imagined
19.	__ A T __ __ __ __	Grew older or more ripe
20.	__ __ __ __ __ A T	Percussionist's regular pulse
21.	__ __ __ __ __ __ A	Atlantic island
22.	__ A __ __ __ __	Wireless headphone
23.	__ __ A __ __	Facial hair
24.	__ __ A __	Small glass sphere
25.	__ __ __	Sleeping place
26.	__ __	Exist

B

102

Place the answers to the questions, letter by letter, into the numbered boxes. Then move the letters into their corresponding boxes in the coded message below to reveal a famous quote from the Second World War.

1. What is the surname of Jeremy, the actor who portrays Hawkeye in the *Avengers* film series?

1 __ 2 __ 3 __ 4 __ 5 __ 6 __

2. Which Dickens novel is set partly in London and partly in Paris?

7 __ 8 __ 9 __ 10 __ 11 __ 12 __ 13 __ 14 __ 15 __ 16 __ 17 __
18 __ 19 __ 20 __ 21 __ 22 __

3. What is the largest creature ever to have lived?

23 __ 24 __ 25 __ 26 __ 27 __ 28 __ 29 __ 30 __ 31 __

4. In computing, what is the process of selecting text on a page known as?

32 __ 33 __ 34 __ 35 __ 36 __ 37 __ 38 __ 39 __ 40 __ 41 __ 43 __

5. What famous London thoroughfare runs from Piccadilly to Oxford Circus?

44 __ 45 __ 46 __ 47 __ 48 __ 49 __ 50 __ 51 __ 52 __ 53 __ 54 __ 55 __

6. What is the French for "cake", used in English for an especially fine dessert?

56 __ 57 __ 58 __ 60 __ 61 __

7. Mole, Rat, Badger, and Toad are characters in what classic children's novel?

62 __ 63 __ 64 __ 65 __ 66 __ 67 __ 68 __ 69 __ 70 __ 71 __ 72 __
73 __ 74 __ 75 __ 76 __ 77 __ 78 __ 79 __ 80 __ 81 __

8. The adjective hepatic relates to which organ of the body?

81 __ 82 __ 83 __ 84 __ 85 __

9. Of what does a bass guitar have four; a harp 47; and Pinocchio zero?

86 __ 87 __ 88 __ 89 __ 90 __ 91 __ 92 __

10. How is the murderous horseman in the story *Sleepy Hollow* described?

93 __ 94 __ 95 __ 96 __ 97 __ 98 __ 99 __ 100 __

11. What word for food prepared in line with Islamic law means "permissible" in Arabic?

101 __ 102 __ 103 __ 104 __ 105 __

12. What item of sewing equipment would a belonephobic person fear?

106 __ 107 __ 108 __ 109 __ 110 __ 111 __ 112 __

"65 __ 84 __   99 __ 32 __ 7 __ 77 __ L

F20 __ 34 __ 101 __ 8 __   12 __ 106 __   55 __ H26 __

23 __ 98 __ 57 __ 17 __ 72 __ 59 __ S,   27 __ 64 __

86 __ H102 __ 24 __ 103 __   F89 __ 46 __ 39 __ 49 __

78 __ 3 __   14 __ 63 __ 31 __

L60 __ 70 __ D66 __ 48 __ 56 __

43 __ 85 __ 16 __ 61 __ 4 __ D112 __ ,   74 __ 73 __

92 __ H95 __ 81 __ 97 __   F82 __ 38 __ H87 __   33 __ 67 __

58 __ 93 __ 47 __   13 __ 69 __ 53 __ 105 __ 96 __ 100 __

9 __ N109 __   37 __ N 40 __ H11 __

S51 __ 6 __ 108 __ 54 __ 71 __ S,   15 __ 107 __

S28 __ 29 __ 30 __ 110 __   F75 __ 91 __ 35 __ 19 __   18 __ N

62 __ H45 __   H41 __ 10 __ 76 __ 50 __ ;   79 __ 94 __

80 __ H104 __ L36 __   90 __ 2 __ 83 __ 111 __ 1 __

22 __ 24 __ 44 __ 88 __ 21 __ 42 __ 68 __ 5 __ 52 __ . "

103

Can you find a home for all these chemical elements in the crisscross grid below?

3 letters
Tin

4 letters
Gold
Iron
Lead
Zinc

5 letters
Argon
Boron
Radon
Xenon

6 letters
Barium
Cobalt
Nickel
Osmium
Silver

7 letters
Bismuth
Bohrium
Bromine
Gallium
Mercury
Silicon

8 letters
Lutetium
Nihonium
Nobelium
Tantalum
Tungsten

9 letters
Manganese
Plutonium
Potassium

10 letters
Molybdenum
Promethium
Seaborgium

11 letters
Einsteinium
Mendelevium

13 letters
Rutherfordium

104

■	18	■	17	■	12	■	15	■	17	■	20	■
24	7 N	18 I	19 Q	24	13	■	13	1	22	15	2	10
■	7	■	24	■	14	■	14	■	18	■	24	■
25	2	11	13	■	20	13	17	6	12	18	21	13
■	■	■	14	■	18	■	26	■	18	■	26	■
5	14	15	11	18	7	16	■	17	26	24	23	23
■	12	■	■	■	16	■	21	■	■	■	24	■
5	12	14	22	17	■	15	18	16	3	26	15	10
■	14	■	12	■	5	■	16	■	2	■	■	■
17	7	13	13	9	18	7	16	■	22	18	16	17
■	16	■	23	■	4	■	13	■	18	■	2	■
12	13	26	18	12	13	■	17	18	7	16	15	13
■	20	■	8	■	17	■	26	■	16	■	23	■

A B C D E F G H I J K L M N O P Q R S T U V W X Y Z

1	2	3	4	5	6	7	8	9	10	11	12	13
14	15	16	17	18	19	20	21	22	23	24	25	26

105

This wordsearch celebrates the movies of Oscar-nominated actress Helena Bonham Carter. How many of her performances can you find in the grid below?

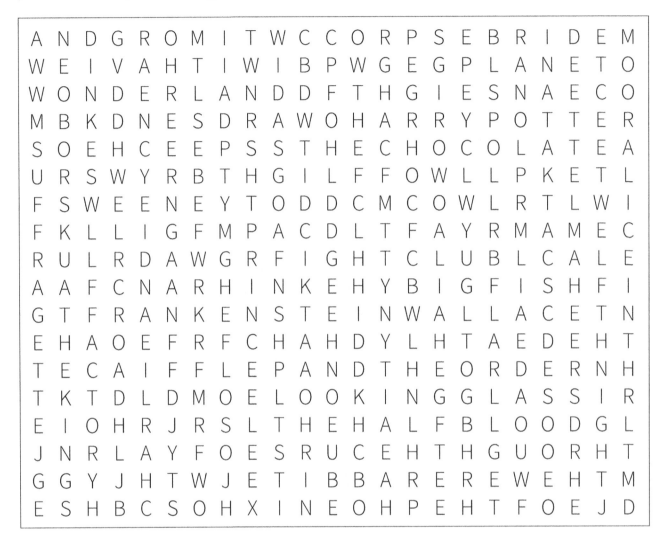

```
A N D G R O M I T W C C O R P S E B R I D E M
W E I V A H T I W I B P W G E G P L A N E T O
W O N D E R L A N D D F T H G I E S N A E C O
M B K D N E S D R A W O H A R R Y P O T T E R
S O E H C E E P S S T H E C H O C O L A T E A
U R S W Y R B T H G I L F F O W L L P K E T L
F S W E E N E Y T O D D C M C O W L R T L W I
F K L L I G F M P A C D L T F A Y R M A M E C
R U L R D A W G R F I G H T C L U B L C A L E
A A F C N A R H I N K E H Y B I G F I S H F I
G T F R A N K E N S T E I N W A L L A C E T N
E H A O E R F C H A H D Y L H T A E D E H T
T E C A I F F L E P A N D T H E O R D E R N H
T K T D L M O E L O O K I N G G L A S S I R
E I O H R J R S L T H E H A L F B L O O D G L
J N R L A Y F O E S R U C E H T H G U O R H T
G G Y J H T W J E T I B B A R E R E W E H T M
E S H B C S O H X I N E O H P E H T F O E J D
```

A room / with a view

Alice in / wonderland

Harry potter / and the order / of the phoenix

Big fish

Charlie and / the chocolate / factory

Cinderella

Corpse bride

Fight club

Frankenstein

Hamlet

Howards end

Through the / looking glass

Ocean's eight

Planet / of the apes

Suffragette

Sweeney todd

The deathly / hallows

The half-blood / prince

The king's / speech

The theory / of flight

Twelfth night

Wallace / and gromit / the curse of / The were-rabbit

❶ DID YOU KNOW?

Helena Bonham Carter is a distant cousin to the Duchess of Cambridge, Kate Middleton.

106

Can you decode this cryptogram to spell out a famous bit of proverbial advice?

E G H   E   G U Y Y O   N T L G X U Z D
E D B   O Z T ' Y Y   A L X   E   G U Y Y O E D G J L W

_S_ _ S_ _ _Y _ _ _S_ _ _N

_N_ Y_ _'_ _ _ _ _ _ S_ _ _Y _NS_ _ _

107

Each of the answers to the 12 questions in this tricky quiz begins with the final two letters of the previous answer. Can you use that hint to answer them all?

1. What is the liquid component of human blood called?
2. Which American poet and novelist who died in 2014 wrote the famous 1969 memoir *I Know Why the Caged Bird Sings*?
3. What is the name of Microsoft's email service?
4. What classic Rodgers and Hammerstein musical opens with the song "Oh, What a Beautiful Mornin' "?
5. What Californian beach resort, 30 miles from Los Angeles, is known for being home to many Hollywood celebrities?
6. The Seven Factors of Awakening are a set of principles in which major world religion?
7. Founded in 1846, what is the name of the vast complex of museums and educational institutes located in Washington DC?
8. Because it is so cold that it does not rain, what giant polar continent is technically the world's largest desert?
9. What natural stimulant is found in tea and coffee?
10. In what month is Groundhog Day celebrated in the US?
11. What famous golf competition is held every two years between competing European and American teams?
12. What was the title of Mark Ronson and Bruno Mars' 2014 hit single, which became one of the first music videos to have more than four billion views on YouTube?

108

Place the answers to the clues on the right into the corresponding rows in the grid on the left, and a classic American novel will be spelled out in the shaded column.

1. A maker of menswear
2. Capital of Canada
3. Martial art
4. Bring in produce from abroad
5. Ancient measure of distance, equal to three miles
6. Attorney
7. On every occasion
8. Portable; a cellular telephone
9. Product; yield of a process or investment
10. Bird known for its two-tone call
11. Royal, regal
12. Bluish-purple dye
13. Required
14. Shows the way
15. Higher quality; recovered from a period of sickness
16. Wants to scratch
17. Modern; not long gone
18. Whilst

#					
1			L		R
2					A
3	A	R			
4	M			R	
5				U	E
6		Y			
7				Y	
8	O			L	
9		T			T
10				O	O
11	I				Y
12					O
13	E	E			
14		I			S
15		T			
16			H		
17		C			
18					G

109

Can you figure out what these 10-letter words are given from a few of their letters?

1. _ _ G H _ H _ _ _ E
2. _ _ N _ G _ M _ N _
3. _ _ C H N _ _ _ _ Y
4. _ _ O D C H _ _ _ S
5. W _ _ _ _ P _ _ _ F

110

Place the answers to the questions, letter by letter, into the numbered boxes. Then move the letters into their corresponding boxes in the coded message below to reveal the opening verse of a famous poem.

1. What structure is the oldest crossing of the East River in New York City?

1 __ 2 __ 3 __ 4 __ 5 __ 6 __ 7 __ 8 __ 9 __ 10 __ 11 __ 12 __

13 __ 14 __

2. What language would be spoken in a hispanophone country?

15 __ 16 __ 17 __ 18 __ 19 __ 20 __ 21 __

3. What Olympic track and field event comprises seven athletic disciplines?

22 __ 23 __ 24 __ 25 __ 26 __ 27 __ 28 __ 29 __ 30 __ 31 __

4. Tins of what food gives Pop-Eye his super strength?

32 __ 33 __ 34 __ 35 __ 36 __ 37 __ 38 __

5. What southeast Asian citrus fruit is the largest in the grapefruit family?

39 __ 40 __ 41 __ 42 __ 43 __ 44 __

6. What name is given to the living timber of a tree below the bark and surrounding the central heartwood?

45 __ 46 __ 47 __ 48 __ 49 __ 50 __ 51 __

7. What is the target score in a game of blackjack?

52 __ 53 __ 54 __ 55 __ 56 __ 57 __ 58 __ 59 __ 60 __

8. What did the poet John Keats describe as the "season of mists and mellow fruitfulness" in a famous poem of 1820?

61 __ 62 __ 63 __ 64 __ 65 __ 66 __

9. Which planet is named after the Roman god of the sea?

67 __ 68 __ 69 __ 70 __ 71 __ 72 __ 73 __

10. What French word for a man's hairpiece is related to the English word "top"?

74 __ 75 __ 76 __ 77 __ 78 __ 79 __

11. What sweet treat is made by melting butter into caramelized sugar?

80 __ 81 __ 82 __ 83 __ 84 __ 85 __

12. What have you just done if you have "oscitated"?

86 __ 87 __ 88 __ 89 __ 90 __ 91 __

"27 __ 38 __ 23 __   4 __ 53 __ 43 __   A66 __ D

25 __ 28 __ E   69 __ 76 __ 20 __ 45 __ 7 __ 37 __ A52 __

88 __ 42 __ 18 __ 63 __   74 __ 30 __   32 __ 85 __ 87 __ /

34 __ 89 __ A   9 __ 54 __ 61 __ 62 __ 56 __ I82 __ 64 __ 6 __

24 __ E17 __ -13 __ 10 __ 68 __ E55 __   1 __ 75 __ 46 __ T. /

80 __ 22 __ 90 __ Y   T3 __ 81 __ 5 __   15 __ O65 __ 60 __

21 __ 58 __ 67 __ E57 __ ,   A72 __ 12 __

39 __ 29 __ 14 __ 59 __ 70 __ 86 __   40 __ F

41 __ 49 __ 35 __ 79 __ Y / 48 __ 2 __ 36 __ 77 __ 47 __ 84 __ 51 __

71 __ 16 __   11 __ N   26 __   83 __ 19 __ V78 __

33 __ 44 __ U31 __ 91 __   8 __ 50 __ T73 __ . "

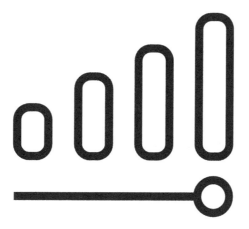

EXPERT

Harder words. More lateral thinking. Mind-bending jumbles.
Here are 10 final puzzles that push the challenges even further!

111

This is a challenging wordsearch with lots of overlaps! All 30 of the words inside it have nine letters, four of which are the letter E. How many of them can you find? It won't be E-asy!

```
C R E E P E R E D E V L E B H
M E D E X C E E D E R S D M N
F L E S S N D E F E R E N C E
R E H R N E B E E K E E P E R
E E C E G R S C R P E B E D I
M T E B W E G E E R E N W R E
E N E E S F R N G E F E P E Y
R E S E Z E E R F E R D L E E
G G E J L R E E E E S E G N O
E D B E S V A B H T V I K T P
N H A B E T L W F E H A E E E
C S E Z E E R F N E H T O R N
E A L R S E L S E W H E R E E
K S I W V F E V E R W E E D R
A F R E E S H E E T W D U C H
```

Beefeater	Creepered	Elsewhere	Everwhere	Genteeler
Beekeeper	Deepeners	Emergence	Exceeders	Reentered
Bejeebers	Deference	Enfeebles	Eyeopener	Reference
Belvedere	Eisegeses	Enfreezes	Feverweed	Refreezes
Beseeched	Elevenses	Evergreen	Freesheet	Rerelease

ⓘ DID YOU KNOW?

The letter E is the most frequently used letter in the English language?
On average, you'll find one in every nine letters of written language!

7	1	5	8	■	16	3	17	10	20	3	3	8
13	■	1	■	11	■	19	■	18	■	23	■	3
11 C	1	12	25	1	8	3	■	7	13	11	1	18
24 K	■	13	■	18	■	■	■	3	■	10	■	15
5 W	6	18	15	8	22	1	3	9	15	8	■	■
13 A	■	■	■	3	■	15	■	1	■	3	■	15
16	10	18	■	14	10	3	10	3	■	8	1	16
15	■	1	■	10	■	13	■	19	■	■	■	13
■	■	5	22	3	3	9	7	13	16	16	1	5
20	■	22	■	18	■	■	■	7	■	13	■	1
13	20	3	18	26	■	7	1	9	9	1	1	18
4	■	16	■	9	■	13	■	3	■	8	■	20
3	19	3	16	21	1	18	3	■	2	3	26	8

A B C D E F G H I J K L M N O P Q R S T U V W X Y Z

1	2	3	4	5	6	7	8	9	10	11	12	13
14	15	16	17	18	19	20	21	22	23	24	25	26

113

You can expect lots of overlaps in this puzzle, so make sure you find your way through it correctly! All of the eight-letter words that fit in this grid contain a consecutive A and Z. Can you find a home for all 33 words?

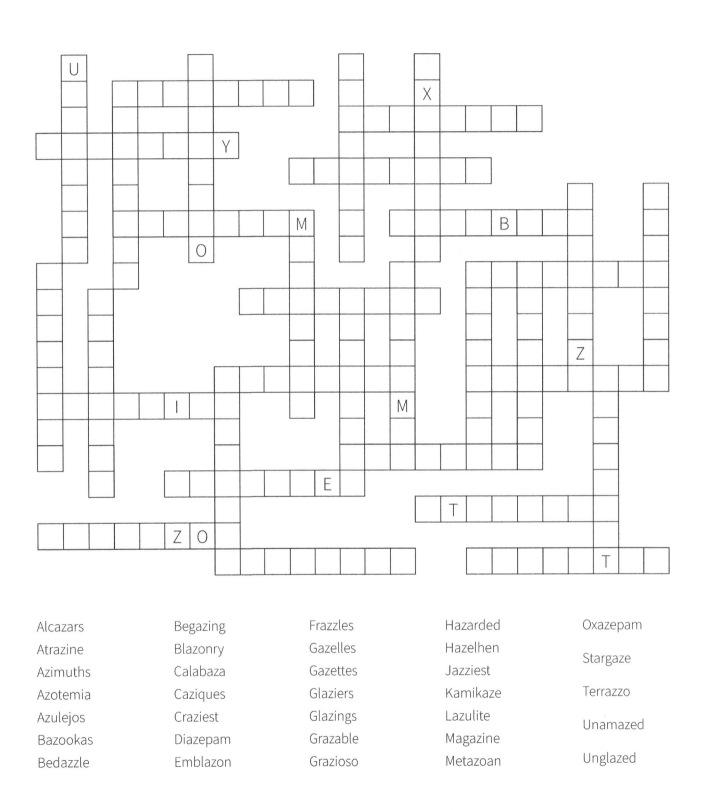

Alcazars	Begazing	Frazzles	Hazarded	Oxazepam
Atrazine	Blazonry	Gazelles	Hazelhen	Stargaze
Azimuths	Calabaza	Gazettes	Jazziest	
Azotemia	Caziques	Glaziers	Kamikaze	Terrazzo
Azulejos	Craziest	Glazings	Lazulite	
Bazookas	Diazepam	Grazable	Magazine	Unamazed
Bedazzle	Emblazon	Grazioso	Metazoan	Unglazed

114

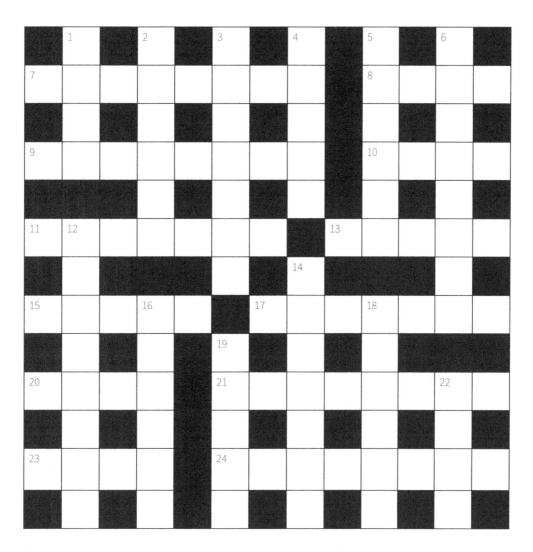

Across

1. Pink waterbird (8)
8. Soothe (4)
9. Made sure a rule was followed (8)
10. Encounter (4)
11. Reuse (7)
13. Extremely angry (5)
15. Rose to your feet (5)
17. Travel hub (7)
20. Visage (4)
21. Puts on display (8)
23. Computer symbol (4)
24. Pinching (8)

Down

1. Baked pie or tart (4)
2. Personify (6)
3. Finger joint (7)
4. Noisy, boisterous (5)
5. Former graduates (6)
6. Secret, like a motive (8)
12. Way of getting in (8)
14. Combatant, boxer (7)
16. Vast seas (6)
18. Small stone (6)
19. Wild animal (5)
22. Noticeable taste (4)

115

Here's a trickier acrostic challenge for you…No letters are filled in to get you started, but there are TWO downward answers to uncover—one reading down the shaded column as usual, and another spelled out line by line in the uneven boxes to the right. Both are the titles of movies released in the 2010s. Can you figure them both out?

1. A casual, quickly taken photograph

2. Country where the Algarve is a popular tourist area

3. Show the way

4. Hard, dreary, monotonous work

5. Feelings

6. Limit access to; confine

7. French-speaking city in Canada

8. First animal listed in a standard dictionary

9. Emery board

10. Decorative water feature

11. Relics, old valuable artifacts

12. Answer, reply

13. Inglenook

14. Amorous, tender

15. Abroad

16. Michael Jackson's famous backward dance move

17. Lingering, like a ghost

18. Someone who watches or witnesses

19. Errors

20. Imagine, picture in your mind

#							
1	N						
2	O						
3	N						
4	R						
5	M						
6	E						
7	O						
8	A						
9	A						
10	O						
11	N						
12	E						
13	I						
14	O						
15	V						
16	O						
17	A						
18	B						
19	I						
20	N						

116

Place the answers to the questions, letter by letter, into the numbered boxes. Then move the letters into their corresponding boxes in the coded message below to reveal a famous quote from Shakespeare.

1. What two numbers are you said to be "at" if you're muddled or confused?

1 __ 2 __ 3 __ 4 __ 5 __ 6 __ 7 __ 8 __ 9 __ 10 __ 11 __ 12 __

13 __ 14 __

2. According to the Bible, where was Jesus born?

15 __ 16 __ 17 __ 18 __ 19 __ 20 __ 21 __ 22 __ 23 __

3. What metallic element has the chemical symbol Ag?

24 __ 25 __ 26 __ 27 __ 28 __ 29 __

4. What famous 1947 play by Tennessee Williams features the characters Stanley Kowalski and Blanche Dubois?

30 __ 31 __ 32 __ 33 __ 34 __ 35 __ 36 __ 37 __ 38 __ 39 __ 40 __

41 __ 42 __ 43 __ 44 __ 45 __ 46 __ 47 __ 48 __ 49 __ 50 __

5. The name of what ancient flying creature literally means "wing-finger"?

51 __ 52 __ 53 __ 54 __ 55 __ 56 __ 57 __ 58 __ 59 __ 60 __ 61 __

6. What major line of longitude is abbreviated to the IDL?

62 __ 63 __ 64 __ 65 __ 66 __ 67 __ 68 __ 69 __ 70 __ 71 __

72 __ 73 __ 74 __ 75 __ 76 __ 77 __ 78 __ 79 __ 80 __ 81 __ 82 __

7. With what sport are the names Pete Sampras and Lleyton Hewitt associated?

83 __ 84 __ 85 __ 86 __ 87 __ 88 __

8. What political term is given to a group of owls?

89 __ 90 __ 91 __ 92 __ 93 __ 94 __ 95 __ 96 __ 97 __ 98 __

9. What is the hard white coating of a tooth called?

99 __ 100 __ 101 __ 102 __ 103 __ 104 __

10. What first name links Colvin, the Grammy winning singer of Sonny Came Home, and Mendes, the Grammy-nominated singer of "In My Blood"?

105 __ 106 __ 107 __ 108 __ 109 __

11. What name is given to an alloy of mercury and another metal?

110 __ 111 __ 112 __ 113 __ 114 __ 115 __ 116 __

12. What is the proper name for a short dash, - , used as a punctuation mark?

117 __ 118 __ 119 __ 120 __ 121 __ 122 __

13. Accra is the capital of what West African country?

123 __ 124 __ 125 __ 126 __ 127 __

14. In the arcade game *Pac-Man*, what are Blinky, Pinky, Inky and Clyde?

128 __ 129 __ 130 __ 131 __ 132 __ 133 __

" 30 _ 104 _ 74 _   52 _ 18 _ 12 _

108 _ 130 _ 29 _ 113 _ 75 _ '133 _   6 _

24 _ 32 _ 107 _ 114 _ 43 _,   90 _ 109 _ 44 _

110 _ 26 _ 79 _   83 _ H 4 _   111 _ 34 _ 126 _

101 _ 63 _ 8 _   W 71 _ 42 _ 99 _ 13 _

23 _ 53 _ 39 _ 22 _ 92 _ Y

89 _ 61 _ 41 _ 118 _ 121 _ 54 _ 5 _ :   64 _ 117 _ 16 _ Y

106 _ 38 _ 11 _ 65 _   98 _ 21 _ 84 _ 80 _ 33 _

96 _ 3 _ 93 _ 77 _ S   73 _ 100 _ 56 _

36 _ 129 _ 78 _ 2 _ 49 _

20 _ 81 _ 132 _ 66 _ 68 _ 67 _ 37 _ 35 _ 105 _ ;

57 _ 72 _ 45 _   55 _ 122 _ 82 _   116 _ 76 _ 7 _

25 _ 86 _   120 _ 62 _ 131 _   17 _ 87 _ 95 _ 28 _

51 _ 19 _ 125 _ 60 _ 14 _   102 _ 94 _ 40 _ Y

119 _ 112 _ 91 _ 69 _ 9 _,   124 _ 48 _ 1 _

127 _ 58 _ 59 _ 88 _   15 _ 50 _ 70 _ 85 _ 123 _

31 _ 103 _ 27 _ 10 _ 97 _   115 _ 128 _ 46 _ 47 _ . "

117

Can you decode this cryptogram to spell out a famous piece of proverbial advice?

GDSSDT SZD XDBKH VNQ EYNC

SZRY SZD XDBKH VNQ XNY'S

_ _ T T _ _ T H _ _ _ _ _ _ _ _ _ _ _ _ _

T H _ _ T H _ _ _ _ _ _ _ _ _ _ _ _'T

118

S

1.	_ _	I am, You are, It _ _
2.	_ _ _	Immoral act
3.	_ _ _ _ _	Trigonometric function
4.	_ _ _ E _	Warning alarm
5.	_ R _ _ E _	Roused, woken up
6.	_ R _ _ _ _ _	Poisonous element As, no. 33
7.	_ _ _ _ _ _ R E	Dermatological treatments
8.	_ R _ _ _ E _ _	Most bad-tempered
9.	R E _ _ _ _ _ _ _	Organizing or piling up again
10.	_ _ _ _ _ E _ R _ _ _	Narrow mountain-biking trail

119

The answers to these seven questions all have something in common. Can you work out what the connection is for a bonus point?

1. In what simple guessing game do players use "their little eye" to spot things?

2. In what 2006 film did Hugo Weaving play a masked vigilante?

3. Storm, Gambit, Angel, and Colossus are members of what superhero group?

4. The British pound sign, £, is an adaptation of what letter of the alphabet?

5. What is the central key of a piano keyboard called?

6. What was the middle initial of presidents Roosevelt and Eisenhower?

7. What multicolored chocolates were once sold under the slogan, "Melts in your mouth, not in your hand"?

8. What connects these answers?

Here's a wordsearch with one final fiendish twist! All of the words you're looking for have been jumbled up! Given only a clue to their meaning, can you unjumble the anagrams and find all thirty of their nine-letter answers in the grid?

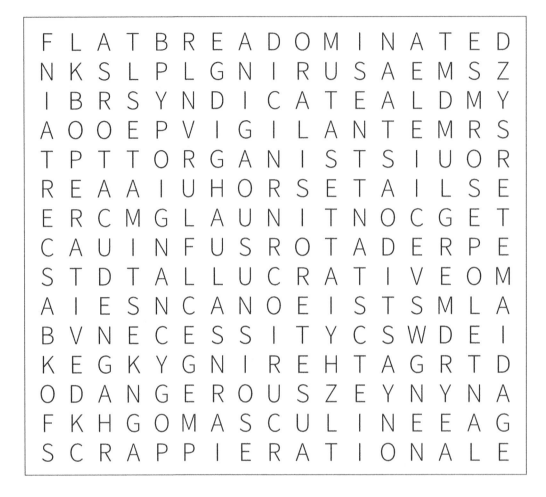

1. Aeroducts (Teachers, tutors)

2. Aeroliths (Dense, grass-like weed; a type of waterfall)

3. Alienator (Justification, meaning behind an action)

4. Assorting (Church keyboardists)

5. Asyndetic (Association, consortium)

6. Calumnies (Male, manly)

7. Canopying (Pathos)

8. Cessation (Kayakers)

9. Cysteines (Need)

10. Demantoid (Overpowered)

11. Draftable (Unleavened snack often served with hummus)

12. Dreamiest (Circular cross sections)

13. Evaporite (In working order)

14. Genitival (Someone who takes the law into their own hands)

15. Geraniums (Gauging, assessing)

16. Inoculant (Incessant, unending)

17. Nightgear (Amassing, collecting)

18. Noseguard (Perilous)

19. Pericarps (Patchier, less finished)

20. Pleonaste (Gazelles)

21. Raunchier (Cyclone)

22. Sectarian (Make sure)

23. Steamiest (Guesses)

24. Teardrops (Hunters)

25. Victualer (Money-spinning)

☀ SOLUTIONS

1

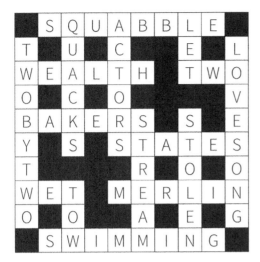

5

2

3

A bird in the hand is worth two in the bush.

4

1. IN
2. GIN
3. GRIN
4. GRAIN
5. REGAIN
6. EARNING
7. GRANNIES

6

A	I	R	P	O	R	T
D	O	L	L	A	R	S
A	U	C	T	I	O	N
M	I	N	U	T	E	S
A	N	I	M	A	L	S
N	U	C	L	E	A	R
D	I	A	M	O	N	D
E	X	P	L	O	R	E
V	I	L	L	A	G	E
E	N	L	A	R	G	E

Hidden phrase: *Pirates of the Caribbean*

7

1. Baboon.
2. Noodle.
3. Trillion.
4. Neutral.
5. Bauble.
6. Flubber.
7. Curb.
Coded phrase: "Double, double, toil and trouble; Fire burn, and cauldron bubble."

8

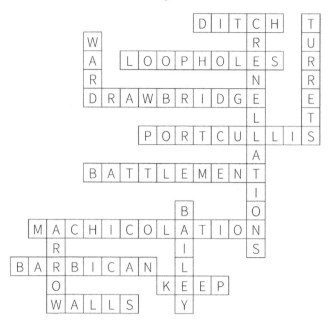

9

1. Bacon

2. Still

3. Total

4. Fairy

5. Input

6. Scene

7. React

Hidden word: OSTRICH

10

1. Italy.

2. Albus Dumbledore.

3. 1910s (1914-18).

4. Rice.

5. A.

6. Bird.

7. Leg.

8. Saturn.

9. Javelin.

10. Henry VIII.

11

P	R	E	S	I	D	E	N	T
I	M	P	O	R	T	A	N	T
R	O	B	I	N	H	O	O	D
A	U	S	T	R	A	L	I	A
T	E	L	E	P	H	O	N	E
E	L	I	Z	A	B	E	T	H
S	E	P	T	E	M	B	E	R
O	B	V	I	O	U	S	L	Y
F	I	R	E	W	O	R	K	S
T	E	D	D	Y	B	E	A	R
H	O	L	L	Y	W	O	O	D
E	M	E	R	G	E	N	C	Y
C	H	R	I	S	T	M	A	S
A	D	V	E	N	T	U	R	E
R	O	A	L	D	D	A	H	L
I	N	T	E	R	V	I	E	W
B	E	G	I	N	N	I	N	G
B	E	E	T	H	O	V	E	N
E	D	I	N	B	U	R	G	H
A	L	E	X	A	N	D	E	R
N	O	R	T	H	E	A	S	T

Hidden phrase: Adam and Eve

12

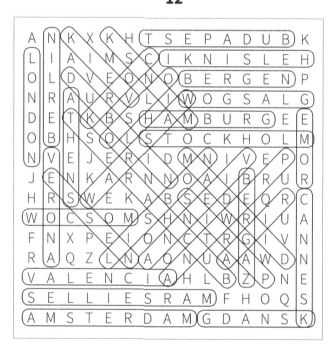

13

16

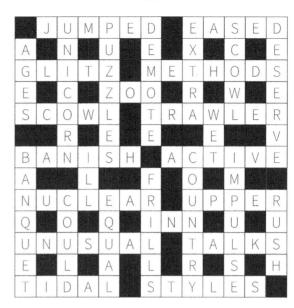

14

A picture is worth a thousand words.

15

1. Bishop. **2.** Bird. **3.** Birch. **4.** Bingo.
5. Bikini. **6.** Binary. **7.** Big Ben.
8. Bicycle. **9.** Billion. **10.** Biology.
11. Big Apple. **12.** Billy the Kid.

17

1. Bears. **2.** Sesame. **3.** Moose. **4.** Ghost town.
5. Mitosis. **6.** Flight. **7.** *The Twits.*
8. White. **9.** Foot. **10.** Fifth. **11.** Ewe. **12.** Adios.
Hidden phrase: "It was the best of times, it was the worst of times, it was the age of wisdom, it was the age of foolishness."

18

19

L	I	T	T	L	E	R
E	V	E	N	I	N	G
A	D	D	R	E	S	S
N	E	I	T	H	E	R
I	R	O	N	A	G	E
N	E	W	Y	O	R	K
G	A	N	D	A	L	F
T	U	E	S	D	A	Y
O	L	Y	M	P	I	C
W	E	S	T	E	R	N
E	X	P	E	R	T	S
R	I	C	H	A	R	D
O	C	T	O	B	E	R
F	R	I	E	N	D	S
P	R	I	V	A	T	E
I	C	E	L	A	N	D
S	I	M	P	S	O	N
A	N	S	W	E	R	S

Hidden phrase: Leaning Tower of Pisa

20

1. I
2. IS
3. SIR
4. STIR
5. TRIPS
6. SCRIPT
7. TRICEPS
8. PICTURES

21

1. EasterN/Never = N **2.** PleasE/Equip = E
3. NoW/When = W **4.** EarlY/Yours = Y
5. PedalO/Orange = O **6.** BreatheR/Ranger = R
7. InK/Knot = K **8.** FirsT/Them = T
9. TaxI/Ideal = I **10.** RealM/Males = M
11. BrowsE/Events = E **12.** DiscusS/Shall = S
Hidden phrase: New York Times

22

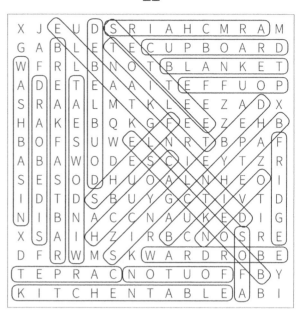

23

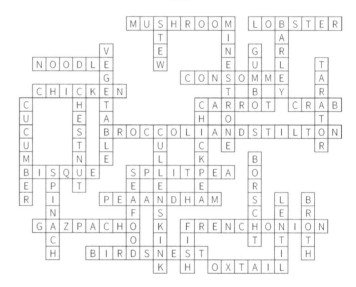

24

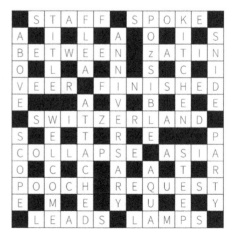

25

1. Moon. **2.** Bieber. **3.** Golf.
4. Decade. **5.** David. **6.** Mandela.
7. Rounders. **8.** Four. **9.** Willow.
10. Tofu. **11.** Horse. **12.** Hedge.

Coded message: "If more of us valued food and cheer and song above hoarded gold, it would be a merrier world."

26

1. Adopt

2. Valid

3. Craft

4. Often

5. Index

6. Comma

7. Music

8. Alter

9. Haste

10. Vivid

11. Eagle

12. Loser

Hidden word: DIFFICULTIES

27

1. Adele. **2.** Paris. **3.** Victoria. **4.** Six. **5.** Nobel Prizes.
6. Egypt. **7.** Badger. **8.** Gallon. **9.** Caribbean. **10.** Cricket.

28

1. Monopoly

2. Cleopatra

3. Mosquito

4. Volcano

5. Weekend

6. Ivory

7. Mountie

8. Andrew

9. Handwriting

10. Faraday

Hidden phrase: "Once upon a midnight dreary, while I pondered, weak and weary, Over many a quaint and curious volume of forgotten lore"

29

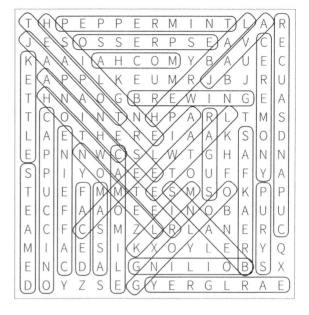

30

J	A	M	E	S
A	C	T	O	R
C	H	I	N	A
K	O	A	L	A
A	N	G	L	E
N	I	G	H	T
D	R	I	N	K
T	H	I	N	K
H	O	T	E	L
E	A	R	L	Y
B	L	A	C	K
E	M	A	I	L
A	N	V	I	L
N	I	C	E	R
S	T	I	C	K
T	O	T	A	L
A	P	P	L	E
L	O	C	A	L
K	I	N	G	S

Hidden phrase: *Jack and the Beanstalk*

31

A	
1. PA	**4.** TAPIR
2. PAR	**5.** PIRATE
3. PAIR	**6.** PAINTER
	7. TERRAPIN

32

An apple a day keeps the doctor away.

33

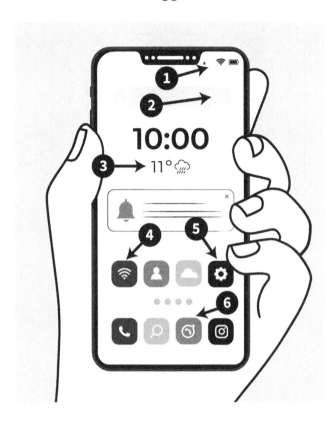

34

1. Pride. **2.** Popeye. **3.** Peregrine.
4. Portuguese. **5.** Palette. **6.** *Pride and Prejudice.*
7. Porsche. **8.** Pancake. **9.** Purple. **10.** Perspective.
11. Prague. **12.** Prince.

35

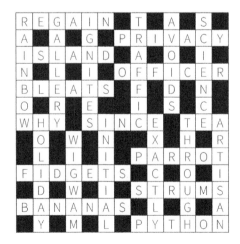

36

T	A	L	E	N	T	
H	A	M	L	E	T	
E	L	E	V	E	N	
M	E	D	I	U	M	
I	C	A	R	U	S	
D	A	N	I	E	L	
D	A	R	W	I	N	
L	A	D	D	E	R	
E	U	R	O	P	E	
O	X	F	O	R	D	
F	U	N	N	E	L	
N	E	W	E	S	T	
O	N	L	I	N	E	
W	H	A	L	E	S	
H	O	U	R	L	Y	
E	N	O	U	G	H	
R	E	T	U	R	N	
E	A	R	W	A	X	

Hidden phrase: The middle of nowhere

37

38

1. The Lord of the Rings. **2.** Teaspoon. **3.** Coronation.
4. Edinburgh. **5.** Boron. **6.** Vincent. **7.** France.
8. Cast Away. **9.** Thirteen. **10.** Souvenir.
Hidden phrase: "Four score and seven years ago
our fathers brought forth, upon this continent,
a new nation, conceived in liberty"

39

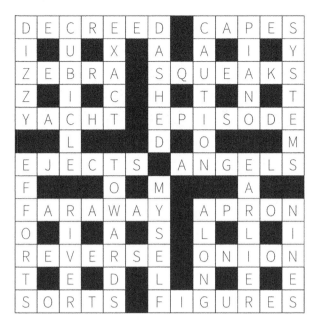

42

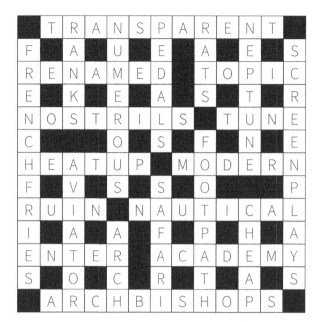

40

Don't count your chickens before they hatch.

41

A	C	C	O	U	N	T
N	I	G	E	R	I	A
T	O	W	A	R	D	S
O	C	T	O	B	E	R
N	A	U	G	H	T	Y
Y	O	U	N	G	E	R
A	V	E	R	A	G	E
N	O	T	I	C	E	D
D	I	S	E	A	S	E
C	U	R	R	E	N	T
L	I	N	C	O	L	N
E	A	R	D	R	U	M
O	R	L	A	N	D	O
P	E	R	C	E	N	T
A	L	L	O	W	E	D
T	I	N	Y	T	I	M
R	U	S	S	I	A	N
A	W	E	S	O	M	E

Hidden phrase: Anthony and Cleopatra

43

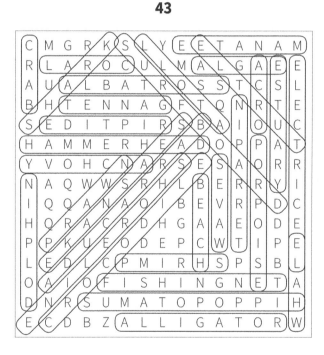

44

E

1. EL

2. ALE

3. SEAL

4. EASEL

5. ASLEEP

6. RELAPSE

7. PLEASURE

45

1. Mango **2.** Apple **3.** Orange **4.** Apricot
5. Banana **6.** Cherry **7.** Grapes **8.** Kiwi

46

47

Don't judge a book by its cover.

48

```
K E Y B O A R D
N I N T E N D O
I N J U R I E S
G A M B L I N G
H O M E W O R K
T H U R S D A Y
S C H E D U L E
O K L A H O M A
F E B R U A R Y
T H A I L A N D
H A R R I S O N
E I N S T E I N
R E Y N O L D S
O R D I N A R Y
U N I V E R S E
N I T R O G E N
D I S T A N C E
T O M O R R O W
A R G U M E N T
B A S E B A L L
L A N G U A G E
E U R O P E A N
```

Hidden phrase: Knights of the round table

49

50

1	+	9	+	16	+	5	**31**
+		+		+		+	
10	+	13	+	12	+	3	**38**
+		+		+		+	
14	+	7	+	6	+	15	**42**
+		+		+		+	
11	+	8	+	4	+	2	**25**
36		**37**		**38**		**25**	

51

1. Iron Man. **2.** Silver.

3. Brass. **4.** Mercury.

5. Tin Man. **6.** Nickel.

7. *David Copperfield.* **8.** Lead.

9. Golden Gate. **10.** Steel drum.

11. Bronze. **12.** All the answers are
or contain the names of metals.

52

53

1. Whittaker. **2.** Saturn. **3.** Ariana Grande.
4. Homophone. **5.** Greece. **6.** Nineteen.
7. Sunspot. **8.** The Dish. **9.** Bandwagon.
10. Headache. **11.** David. **12.** Feta.

Coded phrase: "In the beginning, God created the heaven and the earth. And the earth was without form, and void; and darkness was upon the face of the deep."

54

U	N	T	I	L
U	N	I	E	C	E
I	N	D	I	A
T	H	R	E	E
E	A	G	E	R
D	A	V	I	D
S	T	O	V	E
T	H	E	R	E
A	G	A	I	N
T	W	I	S	T
E	A	G	L	E
S	H	O	R	T
O	N	I	O	N
F	A	L	S	E
A	L	L	O	Y
M	O	T	O	R
E	G	Y	P	T
R	I	V	E	R
I	N	D	E	X
C	H	E	S	S
A	L	I	C	E

Hidden phrase: United States of America

55

56

A
1. AM
2. MAP
3. PALM
4. LAMPS
5. SAMPLE
6. IMPALES
7. MISPLACE

57

The early bird catches the worm.

58

59

60

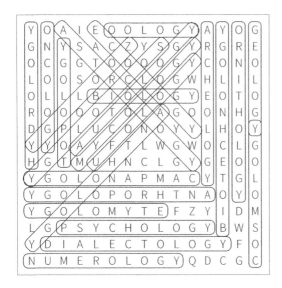

61

A	F	R	I	C	A
S	T	E	V	E	N
F	A	T	H	E	R
A	U	G	U	S	T
R	A	B	B	I	T
A	U	T	H	O	R
S	C	H	O	O	L
T	E	N	N	I	S
H	E	I	G	H	T
E	R	R	O	R	S
E	F	F	O	R	T
Y	E	L	L	O	W
E	E	Y	O	R	E
C	A	N	A	L	S
A	L	W	A	Y	S
N	U	M	B	E	R
S	A	N	D	R	A
E	U	R	O	P	E
E	X	C	E	E	D

Hidden phrase: As far as the eye can see

62

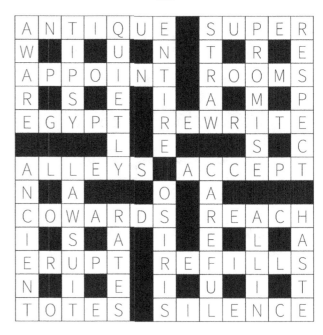

63

1. Jason. **2.** Cauldron.

3. Emma Thompson. **4.** Richard Nixon.

5. Lord Byron. **6.** Bison.

7. Colon. **8.** Cameroon.

9. Nylon. **10.** Lion.

64

1. Crook

2. Nicer

3. Light

4. Water

5. Motor

6. Medic

7. Spook

8. Night

9. Sight

10. Hotel

11. Slink

12. Paper

Hidden word: RELATIONSHIP

65

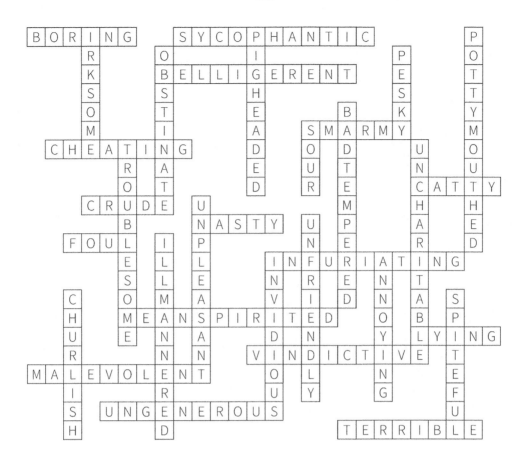

66

A
1. AD
2. BAD
3. BAND
4. BRAND
5. BRANDO
6. BOARD
7. BARD
8. BAR
9. BA

B
10. OB
11. BOO
12. BOOR
13. BORON
14. BRONCO
15. CROON
16. CORN
17. CON
18. CN

C
19. CO
20. COD
21. CORD
22. CROWD
23. COWARD
24. DRACO
25. CARD
26. CAD
27. DA

67

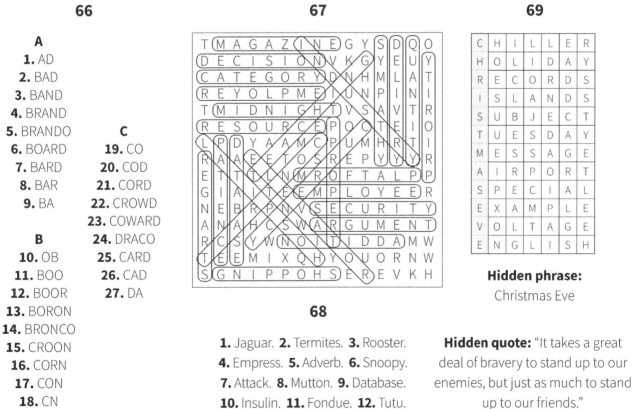

68

1. Jaguar. 2. Termites. 3. Rooster.
4. Empress. 5. Adverb. 6. Snoopy.
7. Attack. 8. Mutton. 9. Database.
10. Insulin. 11. Fondue. 12. Tutu.

69

C	H	I	L	L	E	R
H	O	L	I	D	A	Y
R	E	C	O	R	D	S
I	S	L	A	N	D	S
S	U	B	J	E	C	T
T	U	E	S	D	A	Y
M	E	S	S	A	G	E
A	I	R	P	O	R	T
S	P	E	C	I	A	L
E	X	A	M	P	L	E
V	O	L	T	A	G	E
E	N	G	L	I	S	H

Hidden phrase:
Christmas Eve

Hidden quote: "It takes a great deal of bravery to stand up to our enemies, but just as much to stand up to our friends."

70

```
C H A I N . . G U T
A . J . U S E R . R
L E A S T . A . . I
E . R . S C R U B
N . . . . . . . E
D A N C E . S . S
E . U . R E A L M
R . D O G . N . A
S H E . O R G A N
```

71

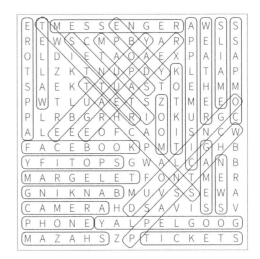

72

73

```
S O M E H O W . W I P E S
A . O . I . . H . I . P
F I N E R . P R I V A T E
E . K . E . I . S . N . A
R E E D S . N E T W O R K
. . Y . . G . L . E
A S S I S T . K E E P E R
C . . U . F . . L . X
C H A M B E R . W H A L E
U . C . H . E . R . T
S Q U E E Z E . O P E R A
E . T . C . L . N . A . C
S P E N T . Y O G H U R T
```

74

Two wrongs don't make a right.

75

S

1. AS
2. SEA
3. SEAM
4. MALES
5. BLAMES
6. MARBLES
7. CLAMBERS
8. SCRAMBLED

76

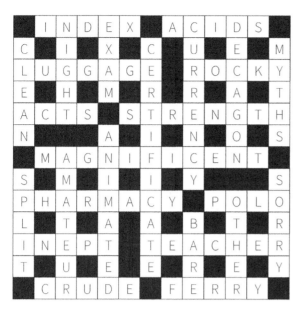

78

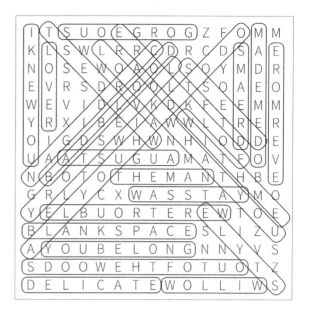

77

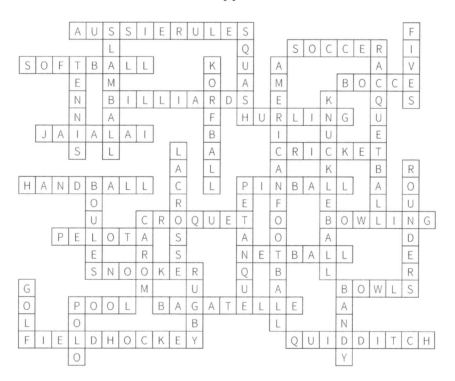

79

You can add
the letters HOW onto
the end of all those
words to spell
ANYHOW,

CHATSHOW,
DOGSHOW,
GAMESHOW,
KNOWHOW,
ROADSHOW,
SIDESHOW,
and SOMEHOW.

80

1. Japan. **2.** Fox. **3.** April.
4. Canada. **5.** Zeus.
6. Scrooge. **7.** George VI.
8. Hotels. **9.** Yeast.
10. Kidneys. **11.** Polo.

12. Qatar. **13.** Xylophone.
14. Martha. **15.** Uranus.
16. Oliver! **17.** Tennis.
18. W. **19.** Vietnam War.
20. Diamonds.
The six unused letters
spell BERLIN.

81

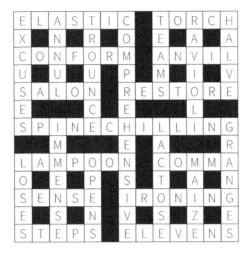

82

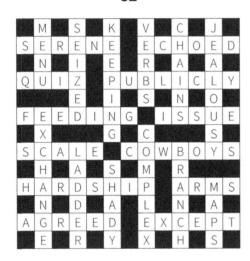

83

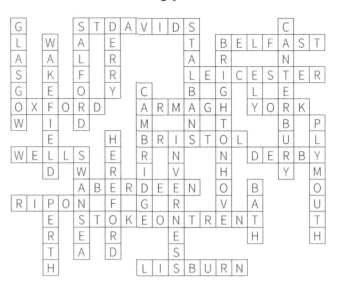

Hidden phrase: Buckingham Palace

84

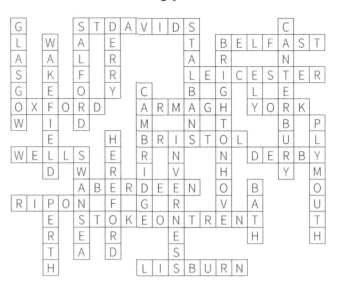

85

The apple never falls far from the tree.

86

1. Midnight. **2.** Omnivore. **3.** Featherweight.
4. Oprah Winfrey. **5.** Horse chestnut. **6.** Peru.
7. Bishop. **8.** Cheese. **9.** Four.
10. Charlotte Bronte. **11.** London. **12.** Atlantic.
13. Camera. **14.** 1950s. **15.** Brought.
16. Paint. **17.** Austria. **18.** Egyptian.
19. Amazon. **20.** Mountain.

87

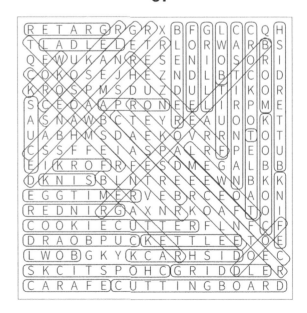

89

B	U	G	S		P	A	S	S	P	O	R	T
I		H			I		P		V			O
B	L	O	O	P	E	R		E	N	E	M	Y
L		S		E			C		R			S
I	N	T	E	R	P	R	E	T	E	D		
C			F				A		U			M
A	B	A	C	U	S		S	C	H	E	M	E
L		L		N			U					S
		A	C	C	O	M	P	L	I	C	E	S
D		B		T		A		O				I
I	D	A	H	O		A	B	R	I	D	G	E
V		M		R		L		E				S
A	N	A	L	Y	Z	E	D		E	D	I	T

90

G	E	N	E	W	I	L	D	E	R
R	E	P	U	T	A	T	I	O	N
E	A	S	T	O	F	E	D	E	N
E	I	S	E	N	H	O	W	E	R
N	O	T	T	I	N	G	H	A	M
B	A	N	G	L	A	D	E	S	H
A	D	A	M	A	N	D	E	V	E
Y	U	G	O	S	L	A	V	I	A
P	A	C	I	F	I	C	R	I	M
A	L	E	X	A	N	D	R	I	A
C	A	L	I	F	O	R	N	I	A
K	I	N	G	S	C	R	O	S	S
E	A	R	T	H	Q	U	A	K	E
R	I	N	G	O	S	T	A	R	R
S	T	O	N	E	H	E	N	G	E

Hidden phrase: Green Bay Packers

91

1. *The Cat in the Hat.* **2.** Indonesia. **3.** Hemsworth.
4. Halloween. **5.** Gall bladder. **6.** Beetroot.
7. Volume. **8.** Fortune. **9.** Arboretum.
10. Metronome. **11.** Pronoun.

Hidden phrase: "O Romeo, Romeo, wherefore art
thou Romeo? Deny thy father and refuse thy name.
Or if thou wilt not, be but sworn my love,
and I'll no longer be a Capulet."

92

I

1. IN
2. NIL
3. LION
4. LOGIN
5. GOBLIN
6. BOWLING
7. ELBOWING

93

A journey of a thousand miles begins with a single step.

94

1. Norway and Finland.
2. George W. Bush and Tony Blair.
3. 64 and 16.
4. Q and P.
5. Atlantic and Pacific.
6. In the morning and in the afternoon (am and pm).
7. Taylor Swift and Ed Sheeran.
8. Mars and Jupiter.
9. T and H.
10. South America and Asia.

95

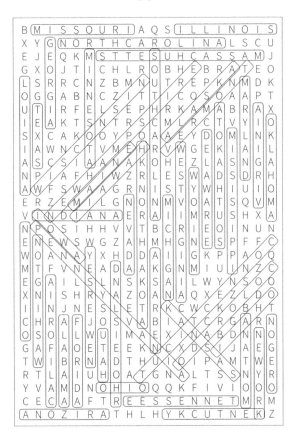

96

97

98

99

100

1. Concentric. **2.** *Othello.* **3.** (Prince) Philip. **4.** Europe. **5.** Nitrogen. **6.** Hammersmith. **7.** Algebra. **8.** Greta Thunberg. **9.** Eve. **10.** Nixon.

BONUS ANSWER: Copenhagen.

101

B	**A**
1. AB	**14.** AT
2. BAT	**15.** ATE
3. BETA	**16.** TEAR
4. BEAST	**17.** RATED
5. ABSENT	**18.** DREAMT
6. BATSMEN	**19.** MATURED
7. BASEMENT	**20.** DRUMBEAT
8. MEANEST	**21.** BERMUDA
9. SEAMEN	**22.** EARBUD
10. NAMES	**23.** BEARD
11. SAME	**24.** BEAD
12. SAM	**25.** BED
13. AS	**26.** BE
	B

102

1. Renner.

2. *A Tale of Two Cities.*

3. Blue whale.

4. Highlighting.

5. Regent Street.

6. Gateau.

7. *The Wind in the Willows.*

8. Liver.

9. Strings.

10. Headless.

11. Halal.

12. Needles.

Hidden phrase: "We shall fight on the beaches, we shall fight on the landing grounds, we shall fight in the fields and in the streets, we shall fight in the hills; we shall never surrender."

103

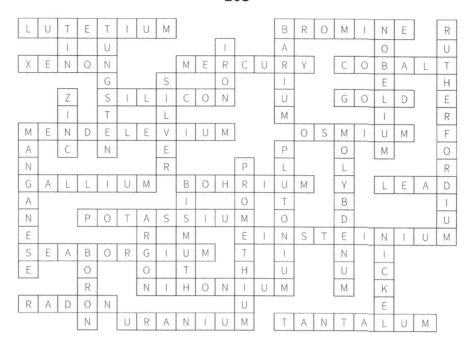

104

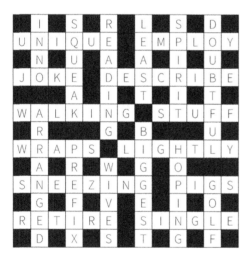

105

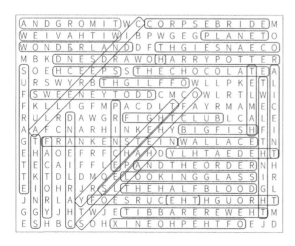

106

Ask a silly question and you'll get a silly answer.

107

1. Plasma. **2.** Maya Angelou. **3.** Outlook.
4. *Oklahoma!*. **5.** Malibu. **6.** Buddhism.
7. Smithsonian. **8.** Antarctica. **9.** Caffeine.
10. February. **11.** Ryder Cup. **12.** "Uptown Funk."

108

T	A	I	L	O	R
O	T	T	A	W	A
K	A	R	A	T	E
I	M	P	O	R	T
L	E	A	G	U	E
L	A	W	Y	E	R
A	L	W	A	Y	S
M	O	B	I	L	E
O	U	T	P	U	T
C	U	C	K	O	O
K	I	N	G	L	Y
I	N	D	I	G	O
N	E	E	D	E	D
G	U	I	D	E	S
B	E	T	T	E	R
I	T	C	H	E	S
R	E	C	E	N	T
D	U	R	I	N	G

Hidden phrase: *To Kill a Mockingbird*

109

1. LIGHTHOUSE
2. MANAGEMENT
3. TECHNOLOGY
4. WOODCHUCKS
5. WATERPROOF

110

1. Brooklyn Bridge. **2.** Spanish. **3.** Heptathlon.
4. Spinach. **5.** Pomelo. **6.** Sapwood.
7. Twenty-one. **8.** Autumn. **9.** Neptune.
10. Toupee. **11.** Toffee. **12.** Yawned.
Hidden phrase: "The Owl and the Pussy-Cat went to sea / In a beautiful pea-green boat. / They took some honey, and plenty of money / Wrapped up in a five-pound note."

111

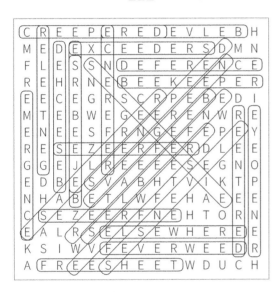

112

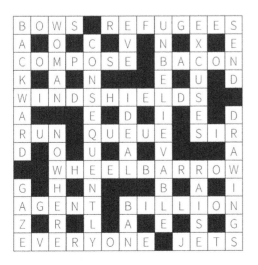

113

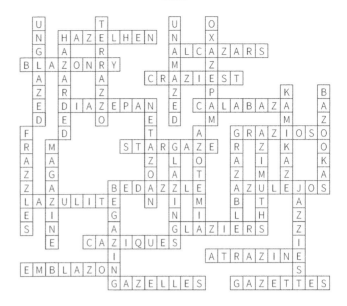

114

115

S N A P S H O T
P O R T U G A L
I N D I C A T E
D R U D G E R Y
E M O T I O N S
R E S T R I C T
M O N T R E A L
A A R D V A R K
N A I L F I L E
F O U N T A I N
A N T I Q U E S
R E S P O N S E
F I R E S I D E
R O M A N T I C
O V E R S E A S
M O O N W A L K
H A U N T I N G
O B S E R V E R
M I S T A K E S
E N V I S A G E

Hidden phrases:

Spider-Man: Far From Home; Star Trek Into Darkness

116

1. Sixes and sevens.
2. Bethlehem.
3. Silver.
4. *A Streetcar Named Desire.*
5. Pterodactyl.
6. International date line.
7. Tennis.
8. Parliament.
9. Enamel.
10. Shawn.
11. Amalgam.
12. Hyphen.
13. Ghana.
14. Ghosts.

Hidden quote: "All the world's a stage, And all the men and women merely players: They have their exits and their entrances; And one man in his time plays many parts, His acts being seven ages."

117

Better the Devil you know
than the Devil you don't

118

1. IS
2. SIN
3. SINE
4. SIREN
5. ARISEN
6. ARSENIC
7. SKINCARE
8. CRANKIEST
9. RESTACKING
10. SINGLE-TRACK

119

1. I Spy.
2. *V for Vendetta.*
3. The X Men.
4. L.
5. Middle C.
6. D.
7. M&Ms.
8. These are the seven letters of the alphabet – I, V, X, L, C, D, and M – that are used as Roman numerals.

120

ANAGRAMS:

1. Educators. 2. Horsetail.
3. Rationale. 4. Organists.
5. Syndicate. 6. Masculine.
7. Poignancy. 8. Canoeists.
9. Necessity. 10. Dominated.
11. Flatbread. 12. Diameters.
13. Operative. 14. Vigilante.
15. Measuring. 16. Continual.
17. Gathering. 18. Dangerous.
19. Scrappier. 20. Antelopes.
21. Hurricane. 22. Ascertain.
23. Estimates. 24. Predators.
25. Lucrative.

Made in the USA
Monee, IL
12 December 2022

21367989R00079